This book has been compiled by the Communisis Million Makers team as part of The Prince's Trust's Million Makers Challenge 2010.

The team is made up of:

Daniella Wainwright

Karen Dudleston

Simon Aitchison

Lucy Bolton

Stacey Clark

Kevin Cook

Sean Hunter

Linda Kennedy

Gary Kingsley

www.thecelebritycookbook.co.uk

Contents

4x5 FILM

The Prince's Trust has one sole aim: To change young lives across the UK. This year we aim to support 44,000 of the hardest-to-reach young people across the country to move forward with their lives.

Through our tailored approach to developing young people's skills, confidence and motivation, eight out of ten of those we help move forward to a positive outcome, such as education or employment.

Communisis are taking part in 'The Million Makers Challenge,' which tasks teams of aspiring entrepreneurs - from graduates to senior employees - to work together to create mini enterprises and raise £10,000 over a six-month period for The Prince's Trust.

I would like to sincerely thank the Communisis team for embracing this challenge and coming up with a truly remarkable product. Million Makers is all about vision, ambition, determination and creativity - all of which the Communisis team have shown in abundance in creating The Celebrity Cookbook.

With best wishes

Julian Barrell
Director of Fundraising
The Prince's Trust

Wale Adeyemi, MBE

I would like to cook for **Richard Branson**, because he's such an inspiring entrepreneur and he would have lots of inspiring and interesting stories to tell. Also, he'd love my cooking.

Thai Chicken Satay

Ingredients
(for 4)

*4 skinless chicken breasts,
cut into thin strips*
Wooden skewers

For the marinade
1 tbsp grated lemon grass
1 small onion
2 cloves garlic
1-2 fresh red chillies, sliced finely
*1 x 2cm piece ginger, peeled
and sliced*
½ tsp dried turmeric
1 tbsp ground coriander
2 tsp cumin
3 tbsp dark soy sauce
3 tbsp fish sauce
5 tbsp brown sugar
1 tbsp fresh lime juice

For the dipping sauce
1 cup roasted peanuts, unsalted
⅓ cup water
1 clove garlic, pressed
1 tsp dark soy sauce
1 tsp sesame oil
2 tbsp brown sugar
2 tbsp fish sauce
½ tsp tamarind paste
1 tsp Thai chilli sauce
⅓ cup coconut milk

Method

Cut the chicken into thin strips and place in a large bowl.

Process all the marinade ingredients in a food processor until smooth.

Pour the marinade over the meat and make sure all the meat is covered. Marinate in the fridge, for at least 1 hour, but up to 24 hours

To prepare the dipping sauce, process all ingredients in a food processor until smooth.

When ready to cook the chicken, carefully thread the meat onto the wooden skewers. Leave space at the end of each skewer, so you can turn the meat later.

Grill the chicken on a medium heat until the chicken is cooked through and the juices run clear. Turn every five minutes during cooking.

> ## " Wale's Cooking Tip
>
> Soak the wooden skewers in water before use to avoid them burning.
>
> You can substitute the chicken for beef, if you prefer. "

Ben Ainslie, CBE

If I could have any role model dead or alive round for dinner, it would have to be **Admiral Lord Horatio Nelson**! I would cook him Beef Wellington which I think Nelson would find appropriate.

Beef Wellington

Ingredients
(for 4)

800g fillet beef

2 tbsp olive oil

250g puff pastry

2 tbsp butter

2 tbsp English mustard

1 tbsp fresh thyme

350g smooth liver paté

1 free range egg

*Salt and ground black
pepper for seasoning*

Method

Pre-heat the oven to 200°C/400°F/
gas mark 6. Place a baking tray
in the oven to warm up.

Heat the oil in a frying pan, then add
the beef. Season with salt and ground
black pepper. Sprinkle the thyme onto
the beef.

Fry briefly, turning in the pan, until all
sides are golden brown – you are only
sealing the beef at this stage.

Remove the beef from the pan and set
aside to cool.

Once cooled, spread the mustard all
over the beef. Then spread the paté over
one side of the beef fillet.

Roll out the pastry, so the sheet is large
enough to completely wrap up the beef.
Place the beef on the pastry sheet, roll
up so the beef is completely enclosed,
pinch close the edges, and then brush
with the egg (beaten).

Chill the Beef Wellington in the fridge
for half an hour, then place on a sheet
of baking parchment, brushed with
the butter.

Place on the pre-heated baking tray
and cook for 30 minutes until the pastry
is golden. The beef should be pink in
the centre.

Serve with your choice of vegetables
and potatoes.

Jane Asher

David Attenborough is my role model, as a man who combines intensive scientific knowledge and professionalism with the gentlest charm and kindness. Even when patiently explaining the irrationality of believing in a beneficent god, he manages to do it without causing offence or hurt: the world would be a far better place if there were more like him. I'd cook slow-braised lamb shanks for him, as he looks like a man who would enjoy a hearty, warming, meaty meal – perhaps when returning home from some far-flung place where he's been living on location catering…

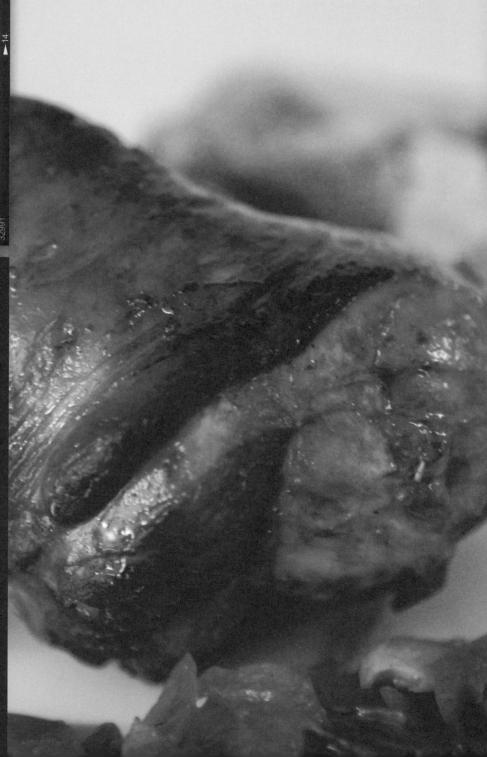

Slow-braised Lamb Shanks

Ingredients (for 4)

4 lamb shanks

1 tbsp olive oil

30g butter

6-8 cloves garlic, peeled

3 red onions, peeled and thickly cut

300ml white wine

100ml water

Dried Provençal herbs (thyme, oregano, rosemary etc)

Handful chopped parsley for serving

Method

Pre-heat the oven to 220°C/425°F/ gas mark 7 (205°C/415°F fan assisted).

Stab the shanks all over with a fork, then rub with salt and black pepper. Melt the butter, together with the oil, in a large pan (preferably one that can be transferred to the oven).

Brown the shanks all over in the hot fat, then add the garlic cloves and red onion, tucking them under the shanks. Cook for a minute or so, being careful not to burn the garlic, then add the dried herbs.

Turn up the heat and add the wine and water and bubble up for a couple of minutes.

Put into the oven, uncovered, for 30 minutes, then turn the heat down to 150°C/285°F/ gas mark 2 (135°C/ 275°F fan assisted), cover the pan and cook for a further 2 to 2 ½ hours.

Transfer the shanks to a serving dish.

Skim some of the fat from the meat juices and discard. Place the pan over high heat and allow the remaining juices to bubble for a couple of minutes until reduced and thickened slightly. Pour over the shanks and sprinkle with the parsley.

Serve with mashed potatoes and a sharply-dressed green salad.

Sasha Behar

I have always been inspired by **Shirley MacLaine**. I love her glamour, her energy, her comic flair, her vulnerability, her fearlessness – her longevity! She feels like a woman who despite having played all these other characters, managed to stay at the centre of her own story pursuing her own passions and bringing them to the world – ever ready though, with a glint in her eye, to kick up her heels and dance. I get the feeling she has really lived her life and is happy to expose the face she has lived it with. I would invite her to tea. We would eat my fantasy chocolate cake – not french and flourless but spongy and full of sweet icing, the kind of thing I am always hoping to stumble across in an Olde English tea room. We would settle down with a cuppa. We would gossip and tell fortunes and she would infect me with enthusiasm again for all of life's possibilities.

Chocolate Cake
(the Olde English tea room kind)

Ingredients

6oz self raising flour

4 eggs

2oz cocoa

8oz caster sugar

8oz butter

2 tsp baking powder

Method

Pre-heat the oven to 180°C/350°F/gas mark 4. Grease two 8 inch sandwich tins. Sift all the dry ingredients together in a mixing bowl. Then add the eggs and butter and beat till light and fluffy.

Bake in the oven for about 25 minutes until the tops are springy to the touch.

Then do what you like icing-wise. Either just fill with buttercream and dust with icing sugar or fill with buttercream and cover top and sides with a darker icing (recipes below).

Buttercream (enough to fill the cake)
Mix about 2oz of butter with 6oz of icing sugar and enough cocoa to make a smooth paste with a tbsp or so of hot water. Voilà.

Dark chocolate icing (enough for top and sides)
Melt 200g dark chocolate with 50g butter. When melted and mixed, stir in one tbsp of coffee.

Put on a lovely, raised cake stand.

Lynda
Bellingham

Here is Lynda's recipe for home-made Victoria Sponge, not from 'Marks & Spencer' as it is in Calendar Girls!

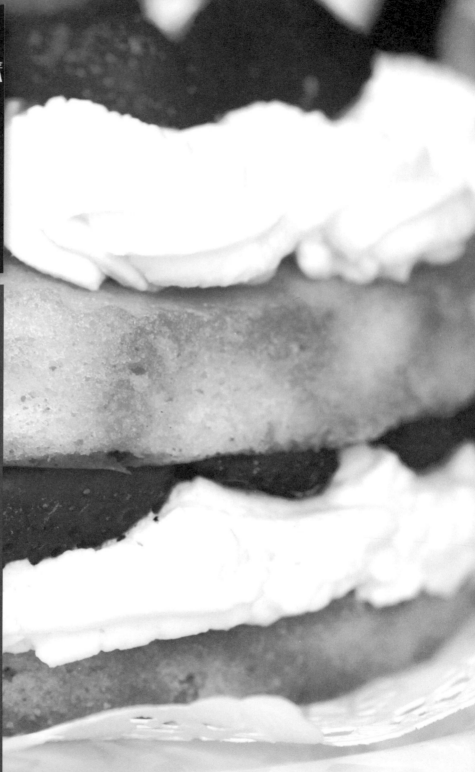

Victoria Sponge

Ingredients

4oz butter

4oz caster sugar

2 large eggs

4oz self raising flour

A few drops of vanilla essence

Whipped cream and strawberries for the filling

Method

Pre-heat oven to 170°C/325°F/ gas mark 3.

Take two 7 inch sponge tins and line with silicone paper.

Mix the butter, sugar and vanilla essence in a bowl until light and fluffy.

Add one beaten egg at a time to the mixture, beating well after each one is added.

Fold in the sieved flour a little at a time with a metal spoon.

Divide mixture equally into the two tins.

Cook in the middle of the oven for about 25 to 30 minutes.

Cool on a wire cooling tray before adding filling and sandwiching together.

Decorate the top with a few of the strawberries and cream.

Eat and enjoy!

© shoot@cameronmcnee.com

Calum Best

My role model would be **Rhonda Byrne** (author of the book 'The Secret').

I would cook a Thai dish which is my favourite kind of food. Maybe prawn tempura to start and miso chicken for main.

Tempura King Prawns with Chilli and Ginger Dipping Sauce

Ingredients
(for 1)

6 large Madagascan prawns

For the batter
125g cornflour
125g plain flour
Pinch of baking powder
Pinch of salt and pepper
250ml ice cold water

For the Dipping Sauce
2cm fresh root ginger
1 clove garlic
2 fresh red chillies, deseeded and finely chopped
1 tbsp fish sauce
100g sugar
100ml red wine vinegar
100ml boiling hot water

Method

Pre-heat a deep fat fryer to 190°C.

To make the batter, sift all the dry ingredients into a bowl.

Add water, mix slowly, folding through with a whisk in an upward motion to make sure it's aerated.

Dip the prawns into the batter and add to the hot oil to cook until the coating browns and crisps.

To make the dipping sauce, blitz all ingredients in a food processor, pour into a serving dish, and serve alongside the prawns.

Calum Best

Miso Chicken with Emerald Vegetables

6 tbsp white/yellow miso paste

3 tbsp runny honey

6 tbsp mirin or dry sherry

6 boneless, skinless chicken thighs

Vegetable oil

2 garlic cloves, peeled and crushed

4 spring onions, cut into 2.5cm pieces

115g extra fine beans, cut into 2.5cm pieces

115g peas, fresh or frozen

Handful of baby spinach, washed

Long grain rice, for serving

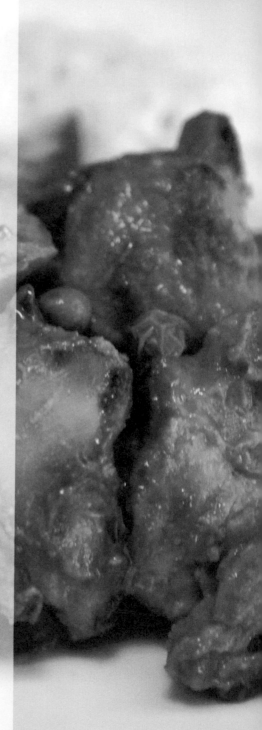

Mix together the miso paste, honey and mirin or sherry. Cut the chicken thighs into 2.5cm pieces and pop them into the miso mixture. Cover and marinade for 20 minutes at room temperature.

Put the vegetable oil in a large frying pan over a medium heat. Remove the chicken from the marinade and fry until golden and cooked through (about 15 minutes). After 10 minutes of cooking, add the garlic and spring onions. Toss to combine.

While the chicken is cooking, heat a small pan of salted water until boiling then cook the beans and peas for 3 minutes.

Drain the vegetables, then add to the cooked chicken with the spinach and the remaining marinade. Toss to combine and cook, stirring occasionally, until the spinach has wilted and the marinade is sticky (about 3 minutes). Serve with plain rice.

Boris Johnson

My role model is **Aristotle** and if he came to dinner I would make him cheese on toast.

Cheese on Toast

Cut a large amount of cheese, preferably cheddar, into slabs.

Lightly toast some brown bread.

Spread toast with butter and chutney.

Cover toast with slabs of cheese.

Grill until it gets all nice and scabby.

© John Shakespeare 2010

Mark Blundell

My role model is **my father** as he has been very instrumental in my life. I would serve him his favourite meal of chilli con carne.

Chilli Con Carne

Ingredients

You will need a slow cooker for this recipe

2lb good quality ground mince beef

1 large onion, finely chopped

4 cloves garlic, chopped

400g can tomato soup

400g tinned tomatoes

2 tbsp paprika

410g can kidney beans, drained

6oz button mushrooms, sliced

1 beef stock cube

1 tsp hot chilli powder

1 tsp cumin

100ml boiling water

Salt and freshly ground pepper

Method

In a large frying pan, add the mince, without any oil, and cook until it crispens slightly. Tip the mince into stoneware and turn onto a low heat.

Add the onion, mushrooms, garlic, soup, tinned tomatoes, paprika, kidney beans, stock cube, chilli powder and cumin. Season and mix well.

Add the boiling water and mix again, then place the lid on top and cook for 4 to 5 hours on a low heat until the meat is tender.

Serve with wholemeal rice or tortillas and sour cream.

Frank Bruno, MBE

www.frankbruno.co.uk

My role model is **Prince Charles**. Away from the public eye he has a real cheeky sense of humour. He is on the level and, with the pressure of his life as a Royal, he certainly gives me inspiration.

Chicken, Rice and Peas with Creole Tomato Salad

Ingredients
(for 4)

For the Chicken, Rice and Peas

8 chicken thighs (or you can use drumsticks or breast meat if preferred)
2 onions, chopped
1 tbsp oil
2 garlic cloves, crushed
1 sprig fresh thyme
1 tbsp all purpose seasoning
2 tbsp lemon juice
1 cup black eyed peas
3 tbsp coconut cream
Enough long grain rice for 4 people

For the Creole Tomato Salad

3 large ripe tomatoes, sliced
1 large red onion, sliced and rings separated
Pinch of salt
2 tsp chopped mint
2 tsp chopped chives
½ clove crushed garlic
1 tbsp olive oil
1 tbsp red wine vinegar
1 tbsp Dijon mustard

Method

Soak the black eyed peas in water overnight.

Next day, pre-heat the oven to 180°C/ 350°F/gas mark 4.

Skin the chicken and ensure all of it is coated with a mixture of salt, lemon juice, 1 chopped onion, 1 crushed garlic clove, and 1 tablespoon all purpose seasoning.

Heat the oil in a frying pan, then add the chicken and fry until golden (you can grill or bake for a healthier option). Transfer the chicken to an ovenproof dish and bake for 30 minutes.

Whilst the chicken bakes, boil the black eyed peas with 1 crushed garlic clove, 1 chopped onion and the thyme sprig. Season well with salt and ground black pepper.

Cook the rice as per the packet instructions whilst the peas are cooking.

When the peas are cooked, drain, and stir in the coconut cream. Add to the drained rice, once this is cooked.

Arrange the sliced tomato on a platter and top with the onion rings.

Sprinkle on the chopped mint, chives, and salt.

Combine the remaining ingredients in a clean jar, replace the top, and shake well to create the dressing.

David Cameron

Italian Sausage Meat Pasta

Fry two chopped red onions in a large deep frying pan. Add the meat squeezed from six spicy Italian sausages. Throw in a handful of chopped rosemary and a seeded and diced red chilli.

Turn up the heat and break up the sausage. Once the meat has broken up and browned, add lots of red wine and reduce. Then add two tins of chopped plum tomatoes.

Reduce the sauce as with Bolognese. Grate loads of Parmesan in a bowl and once the pasta is ready (preferably penne) add together with the Parmesan, half a pint of double cream and the sauce.

© David Jensen

Richard E Grant

Nelson Mandela would be my role model – I was at school in Swaziland with his daughters and in 1975 the prospect of his release and the end of apartheid seemed impossible.

Crab Salad

Pint tub fresh white crab meat

Finely chopped bunch coriander

2 finely chopped medium red chillies

Juice of 3 lemons

1 tbsp Maldon salt

½ pint olive oil

Combine all the ingredients, leave in the fridge for an hour.

Serve with toast and home-made mayonnaise.

Pat Cash

When former Wimbledon champion
Pat Cash is not on the tennis court, there
is nothing he likes more than turning his
talents to the kitchen.

One of his favourite dishes is something
he would prepare for long-term friend and
Iron Maiden lead guitarist **Adrian Smith**,
whose love of sport and life has always
been an inspiration to Pat.

Black Cod
with Yuzu Miso

Ingredients
(for 2)

3 x 200g Black Cod
(bones and scales removed)

75ml sake

75g sugar

150ml mirin

300g white Miso paste

15ml Yuzu juice

1 bamboo leaf (optional)

1 lemon

Method

Heat up sake, mirin and sugar in a saucepan. Flambé very carefully stirring continuously.

Slowly whisk in white Miso paste. Continue to stir.

When the ingredients are well blended, remove from heat and allow the marinade to cool.

Add the Yuzu juice to the marinade and stir.

Remove 1/3 of the marinade and use bottled spring water to thin down.

With the remaining 2/3, marinade the fish for 24 to 36 hours.

Lightly wipe off (with fingers) any excess miso marinade clinging to the fish but do not rinse off.

Place on a bamboo leaf and bake in pre-heated oven at 200°C/400°F/ gas mark 6 for 8 to 10 minutes.

Assembly
Remove fish from the bamboo leaf and place onto plate.

Place one spoonful of the reserved Yuzu sauce next to fish.

Garnish with fresh lemon wedge.

Serve hot.

" Pat's notes

Black Cod, also known as Sablefish in the US, can be hard to source. I find using a sustainable fish such as Salmon the perfect substitute as, like the Black Cod, there is a decent amount of fat in the Salmon allowing the miso flavour to absorb into the fish.

Jaspar
Corbett

www.jasparcorbett.com

My role model would have to be my late father, **John Thalberg Corbett**, who was a man of great fairness and principle.

He died when I was quite young and I would have dearly loved to know him rather better than I did.

Country Pheasant en Croute

Ingredients

Filo pastry

Pheasant breast

500g mushrooms

Knob of butter

2 tsp grainy mustard

284ml double cream

Nutmeg, to taste

1 onion

2 garlic cloves

1 egg yolk

Method

Turn oven onto 180°C/ 350°F/ gas mark 4.

Thinly slice the onion and garlic and pan fry in olive oil until soft. Add the butter and then the pheasant breast until both sides are browned. Leave to one side.

Take a sheet of filo pastry and brush with egg yolk, then spread grainy mustard over the same sheet. Place a second sheet on top and repeat the process. Place the pheasant breast and some of the onion and garlic on the pastry sheets. Now roll the breast in the pastry sheets and egg yolk the finished article. Place on a tray and put in the top of the oven for 12 minutes.

Finely chop the mushrooms and place them in the unwashed frying pan, add more olive oil and a little butter. Sauté these until soft and then add the cream and grate some nutmeg into this.

To serve
First plate the mushrooms and then lay the golden brown pheasant parcel on top – Yum!

As a wine merchant, this dish is of course not complete without a good glass of Vino. Both red and dry white wines go with this dish. However, I would choose a red Burgundy and my preference would be a Pommard.

Dean Edwards

My parents **Steve** and **Vicky** are my role models. From an early age they always encouraged me to cook, and gave me great confidence. But a special mention has to go out to my dad, who was involved in a serious accident last year and is lucky to still be with us!

His recovery will be a long process, but despite contending with both physical and mental challenges, he remains upbeat and positive, and keeps a great sense of humour (always moaning that I don't cook for him enough!).

The way he is dealing with the recovery process is an inspiration to everyone who knows him, and he continues to raise money for both the air ambulance and the burns unit who helped save his life. Strangely, this whole experience has brought the whole family closer together, ensuring we never take life for granted!

Mussels in Cider, Cumin Spiced Lamb with Bombay Potatoes and Mint Raita

Ingredients
(for 2)

Mussels in cider

1kg live mussels

2 shallots finely sliced

3 cloves garlic crushed

100g pancetta lardons

100ml dry cider

2 tbsp flat-leaf parsley chopped

1 tbsp crème fraîche

Black pepper

Ingredients
(for 2)

Cumin spiced lamb with bombay potatoes and mint raita

1 rack of lamb (french trimmed)

3 large potatoes

1 onion

2 cloves garlic

1 fresh chilli

1 tin tomatoes

1 tsp grated fresh ginger

200ml chicken stock

3 fresh tomatoes

Bunch fresh coriander

Bunch fresh mint

½ cucumber

200ml natural yoghurt

2 tsp cumin seeds

2 tbsp mixed whole spices (cumin, coriander, fennel, black peppercorns, mustard seed, cardomon and clove)

Method

Mussels in Cider

Scrub and debeard the mussels. In a pan large enough to fit all of the mussels, fry the pancetta until golden, add the shallots and garlic and continue cooking for 1 to 2 minutes. Add the mussels and cider and cover with a tight fitting lid, steam for 5 to 6 minutes. Stir in the parsley and transfer mussels to a serving bowl with a slotted spoon, discarding any that aren't open. Into the remaining liquor, stir in the crème fraîche and season with black pepper, then pour over the mussels. Serve with some fresh crusty bread.

Method

Bombay potatoes

In a dry pan cook off the whole spices and grind in a mortar and pestle.

Fry finely chopped onion until softened, add ginger and garlic. Add spices and finely chopped chilli. Add tin tomatoes and stock to cover potatoes (peeled, and cut into large chunks).

Cook for approximately 20 minutes. Season with salt, pepper and sugar.

Add freshly chopped coriander.

Lamb

Season and seal lamb in a hot pan and sprinkle liberally with toasted cumin seeds. Transfer to an oven set at 200°C/400°F/gas mark 6 for around 25 to 30 minutes.

Raita

Deseed a cucumber, finely dice and add to yoghurt with some chopped mint and cumin.

Richard Farleigh

As a foster child, I did not have anyone I was naturally close to or that I could call on for advice. I was extremely shy and lacked any confidence. But I was very lucky because at various times in my life different people took me under their wing and frankly, "rescued" me. Some were school teachers, such as **Mrs Walker** who didn't believe that I was backward and got me learning when I was 8 and 9.

My Economics teacher in high school, **Peter Rolfe**, gave me so much encouragement that my school results got better and better. Later, as an investment banker, I was lucky enough to work for **Jillian Broadbent**, a person who combines intellect, humour, charm and tolerance. If only I could be half of what she is. Finally, there is my oldest brother **Rodney Smith**. Fostered at 14 to a series of families, he left school early and was a cleaner working for the railways. By the time he retired, over 30 years later, he was the boss of six of Melbourne's main stations.

This was the winning dish between two mates of mine who each cooked a duck dish, in a battle we called "the Great Duck-Off". He kindly let me nick it!

"DUCK-OFF SALAD"

Ingredients

1 (intact) Peking Duck from Chinese providore

3-4 cups fresh bean sprouts

1 or 2 cucumbers

5-10 spring onions

Bunch of mint and coriander plus 10 kaffir lime leaves

6 limes (cider, palm or white)

Vinegar

Fish sauce

Hoisin sauce

Palm sugar or brown sugar

Fresh bird's-eye or similar hot chillies

Method

Put bean sprouts in colander and pour over a good quantity of boiling water, allow to drain and cool.

Remove all the skin and meat from the carcass of the (cooked) duck; discard all large bits of fat. Shred meat roughly and set aside, do not at any time refrigerate the meat.

Peel and deseed cucumbers and cut into smallish cubes.

Slice spring onions (including the green part) into 1 inch lengths.

Finely chop mint and coriander. De-vein kaffir lime leaves and chiffonade.

Juice 5 limes, slice remaining lime in half and remove all of the central white pith, slice into very fine dice (including rind).

Mix lime juice with an equal amount of vinegar and a splash of fish sauce. Add palm sugar till you have a sweet/sour solution. Add finely chopped chillies to taste. (It should be hot, sweet and sour!)

Keeping a large handful of duck meat aside, combine all of the ingredients until well mixed, drain off excess marinade and dab hoisin sauce randomly over the mixture. Sprinkle remaining duck over the top.

Garnish with extra coriander and serve.

Craig Fitzgibbon

Australian Professional Rugby League player, currently playing for Hull FC

My Role Model: American **Kelly Slater**, 9x World Champion Surfer. Whilst he may not be a household name in the UK, he is a global star and a nine times world champion. I have so much admiration for him and his longevity at the top of his sport. I remember watching him as a starry-eyed teenager and still now he is at the top of his game and still competing for this year's world title (2010).

Any professional sports person will tell you that the hardest thing about being a professional is maintaining a peak level over a long period. Kelly has done this, whilst pioneering changes and evolving as the sport changed around him. It would have been easy for him to walk away at any stage, but he took the hard road and continued, actually winning world titles along the way. The meal I would cook for Kelly Slater is...

Chicken Pad Thai

Ingredients
(for 4)

200g rice noodles

¼ cup sweet chilli sauce

2 tbsp fish sauce

2 limes juiced

2 tbsp coconut oil

2-3 tbsp brown sugar

500g free range chicken breast/thigh fillets

3 spring onions sliced

2 eggs (beaten)

Optional to garnish: chopped peanuts, small chilli, coriander, lime wedges

Method

Put noodles in a large bowl, cover with hot water until softened and white. Drain and rinse under cold water and set aside. Combine chilli sauce, lime juice, fish sauce and brown sugar in a jug. Cut the chicken into strips.

Heat a wok or a large non-stick frying pan over a high heat, add a little of the oil and cook chicken strips in batches until lightly browned, remove from wok and set aside.

Heat remaining oil, stir-fry the spring onions for one minute, add drained noodles to wok and stir until well combined, then add sauce mixture and stir thoroughly. Add the egg, tossing it through all ingredients. Return chicken to wok and cook for 2 to 3 minutes until heated through.

Spoon into serving bowls. Sprinkle with chopped peanuts, coriander leaves and fresh chilli. Serve with lime wedges.

David and Carrie Grant

We would invite **Nelson Mandela** for dinner, because he is so full of wisdom and grace and we're not sure if they have Curried Goat in South Africa!

Curried Goat

Ingredients
(for 6)

4lb goat (easily purchased in large chunks from any halal butcher. If unavailable then mutton is the next best thing)

2 onions – roughly chopped

2 cloves garlic – roughly chopped

2 chillies – roughly chopped

1 can chopped tomatoes

1 tsp mustard

Herbs or 2 bay leaves

½ tsp curry powder

½ tsp paprika for frying

½ cupped hand of paprika (for seasoning goat)

Vegetable oil

¼pt water

Salt and pepper

Method

Heat oil in pan and add:

Onion, garlic, bay leaf or herbs, curry powder and ½ tsp paprika.

Season meat by rubbing in the remaining paprika, salt and pepper. When onions have softened, brown the meat in the oil.

When the meal has been browned add tomatoes, chillies, mustard. To this add water to just under the level of the meat.

Gently cook for 3 hours.

To sweeten add tomato ketchup, if too spicy add 5 tbsp milk.

Christine
Hamilton

Jellied Bloody Mary,
Pan Fried Salmon Fillets with Summer Sauce

Ingredients
(for 12)

Jellied Bloody Mary

1.5l tomato juice

10fl ozs (300ml) Vodka

9 gelatine leaves (or granules but leaves much better)

2 tsp Worcester sauce – more to taste if desired

2 tsp Tabasco sauce – more to taste if desired

2 tsp creamed horseradish – more to taste if desired

Juice of 1 or 2 lemons – approx 6 tbsp

Freshly ground black pepper to taste

To serve

1 tub crème fraîche

1 cucumber

Ingredients
(for 6)

Pan Fried Salmon Fillets with Summer Sauce

4 tomatoes

12 tbsp olive oil

4 tbsp lemon juice

Approx. 10 spring onions finely sliced

6 salmon fillets

Method

Soften gelatine leaves in water and dissolve in small amount of tomato juice.

Put all other ingredients into mixing bowl.

Pour gelatine/tomato mixture in.

Stir well – use hand whisk to break up the horseradish.

Pour into 12 Manhattan/Martini glasses.

You can use ordinary glasses but the Manhattans look stunning.

Leave in fridge until set.

To serve

Mix crème fraîche/yoghurt (or fromage frais) with diced cucumber, garnish with good spoonful on each jelly. Finish with sprig mint/spring onions.

Serve from fridge with good bread. The cool of the creamy topping perfectly balances the fire of the Mary! Leave the Vodka out for teetotallers – but don't invite them again!

These can be made in advance – even the day before – but don't put the creamy stuff on until a few hours in advance. Exact quantities are infinitely variable – except the liquid/gelatine balance of course.

Method

Skin the tomatoes (dip into very hot water for about a minute) and scrape out the seeds. Dice into small cubes.

Place 8 tbsp oil and lemon juice into a small saucepan and heat gently for 2 minutes until warm. Remove from heat and season with salt and freshly ground pepper. Add tomatoes and spring onions.

Heat a little oil in a frying pan over a medium heat, then fry the salmon, skin-side down, for 2 to 3 minutes. Turn over and cook for 3 to 4 minutes until just opaque. Transfer to serving plate and drizzle over the sauce.

Serve with salad or vegetables – garnish with grilled lemon halves.

Ainsley Harriott

It's incredibly soul-searching to decide who would be one's perfect role model. We are often inspired by certain individuals during many different periods in our lives – notably during those early formative years. With this is mind, I'd have to choose the great **Bill Cosby**. From the first time I saw him on the 1960s US television series "I Spy", with Robert Culp, I instantly felt a connection, probably like many other black people around the world. He was the first black American with a major role to act in a drama series and went on to win three consecutive Emmy awards. It made me feel proud and whole, and gave me an inner belief. He's been with us for such a long time and I feel that I've benefited from following his career. Who could forget the great Cosby Show and some of those famous quotes: "Immortality is a long shot – but someone has to be the first." Or my favourite: "Decide that you want it more than you are afraid of it." It would be a pleasure to cook and dine with him, and I'd cook Braised Oxtail with Butter Beans served with crisp buttered green cabbage.

Braised Oxtail with Butter Beans

Ingredients
(for 4)

50g (2oz) seasoned flour

1.5 – 1.75kg (3 – 4lb) oxtail pieces

4 tbsp olive oil

2 onions, chopped

2 carrots, peeled and chopped

2 celery sticks, chopped

Leaves from 3 sprigs of thyme

2 bay leaves

2 cloves garlic, crushed

300ml (½ pint) red wine

1 litre (1¾ pints) chicken stock

1 x 400g (14oz) can chopped tomatoes

1 tbsp tomato puree

1 tbsp Worcestershire sauce

2 x 400g (14oz) cans butter beans, or 1 x 800g (1.75lb) jar, drained and rinsed

Leaves from 0.5 x 20g (0.75oz) packet flat-leaved parsley, chopped

Salt and freshly ground black pepper

Method

Place the seasoned flour in a plastic bag and add the oxtail pieces. Shake until well coated, then remove, dusting off any excess flour. Heat the oil in a large flameproof casserole dish and brown the oxtail pieces in batches. Using a slotted spoon, transfer to a colander and allow the excess oil to drain off.

Add the onions, carrots and celery to the pan and sauté for 10 minutes until softened but not coloured. Add the garlic, thyme and bay leaves and continue to cook for a minute or two. Deglaze the pan with a little of the red wine, scraping the bottom of the pan to release the caramelised juices, then pour in the remainder of the stock, tomatoes, tomato puree and Worcestershire sauce. Season to taste.

Return the oxtail to the pan, bring to the boil, then cover and simmer gently for about 1½ hours, skimming off any fat that bubbles to the surface. Gently stir in the butter beans and continue to cook over a low heat for a further 45 minutes to 1 hour until the meat starts to come away from the bone. Season to taste, scatter with the parsley and serve.

Extracted from Ainsley Harriott's Friends and Family Cookbook, published by BBC Books

Amanda Holden

It's an odd thing, but I don't really have a role model, as I believe everyone's the same, but I have a lot of respect for my peers and take advice from them. I respect other people's opinions but it's my little family that counts most!

PS. I'd have Bill Nighy round to eat my pesto pasta any day!

Pesto Pasta

Ingredients
(for 2)

300g fresh tagliatelle

200g fresh basil leaves

2 cloves garlic, peeled and crushed

80g pine nuts

50g freshly grated parmesan

240ml extra virgin olive oil

1 tsp salt

Packet tender stem broccoli

Extra parmesan for garnish

2 sheets greaseproof paper

Rolling pin

Blender

Method

Roughly chop/tear the basil.

Place into the blender with the crushed garlic and salt. (I always find it easier to use a blender, being a mum!)

Spread the pine nuts between two sheets of greaseproof paper and roll over them with rolling pin to crush them. Add them to the blender.

Pulse the mixture on medium until it forms a thick paste and remove from blender and place into a bowl.

Add the parmesan and hand mix together with a spoon.

Add the olive oil, a tablespoon at a time, and hand mix it in well.

Bring pan of water to boil and cook pasta for a few minutes until al dente. Drain pasta and then pour the pesto over the pasta and toss gently to mix the pesto in. I always steam some broccoli and put it on top at the end and then add some more parmesan too!

Sir David Jason

If I were to cook a meal for a present-day inspirational figure, I would like to cook for **His Royal Highness The Prince of Wales**.

Not only has he inspired thousands of people to beneficially take part in the Prince's Trust projects for many years now, but I also admire his stance on ecology and nature and his interest in the nation's wellbeing.

Of course, all the ingredients would be organic and probably from my garden – apart from the fish! With a nice glass of wine, I hope my meal would be lovely jubbly!

Sir David Jason's
Lovely Jubbly Fish Pie

Ingredients
(for 4-6)

200g cod

200g smoked haddock

200g salmon

125g peeled, raw prawns

1kg potatoes

1 carrot (grated)

2 sticks celery (grated)

150g cheddar cheese

½ lemon

Salt and pepper

2 tbsp mixed herbs

30g butter

Dash of milk

Method

Peel the potatoes, cut into cubes and put on to boil in lightly salted water.

Whilst the potatoes are boiling, place the grated carrot and celery into a pie dish.

Pre-heat the oven to 200°C/400°F/ gas mark 6.

Cut the cod, salmon and smoked haddock into chunks and place these on top of the grated carrot and celery.

Next, add the prawns, a sprinkle of mixed herbs, the juice of half a lemon and a pinch of salt and pepper.

Grate the cheese over the top.

Once the potatoes have cooked, drain them and return to the pan. Mash with the butter and milk until smooth.

Spread the mashed potato over the fish and vegetable mixture and place into the pre-heated oven for 40 minutes.

Serve piping hot with salad.

Peter Jones, CBE

Entrepreneur

There's nothing more traditionally British than the great Sunday Roast. A particular favourite of mine, it embodies everything that I think is wonderful about Great Britain. I love the idea of spending the day preparing food carefully and then coming together to enjoy it with family and friends.

My parents, who have been the most incredible support for me, have always cooked a fantastic Chicken Roast Dinner so I would return the favour by cooking my own version with added kick. I might even do the washing up if they're lucky.

The Dragon's version of the Great British Roast – with a spicy twist – I'm in!

Ingredients
(for 4-6)

1 x 1.5-2kg chicken, we like using free-range or organic if possible

1 medium white onion

1 medium red onion

Jamaican Spicy sauce to taste (I like Reggae Reggae Sauce the most)

1 bulb garlic

Olive oil

Sea salt and black pepper

1 lemon

4 carrots

4 parsnips

4 medium sweet potatoes

Knob of butter

1 tsp freshly grated ginger

1 tsp chilli flakes

Method

Start by par boiling the sweet potatoes for 20 minutes.

Pre-heat the oven to 240°C/475°F/ gas mark 9.

Peel the carrots and parsnips and roughly chop them.

Break the garlic bulb into cloves.

Peel and chop the red onion into slices.

Put all the vegetables (except the sweet potatoes, put these to the side for now) and garlic cloves into the middle of a large roasting tray and drizzle with the olive oil.

Drizzle the chicken with olive oil and the spicy sauce (to taste) and season with salt and pepper, rubbing it all over the chicken.

Put the white onion and the lemon inside the chicken's cavity.

Place the chicken on top of the vegetables in the roasting tray and put it into the pre-heated oven.

Turn the heat down to 200°C/400°F/ gas mark 6 and cook the chicken for 1 hour and 30 minutes (it may need a bit longer or shorter depending on your size of chicken).

Take your par boiled sweet potatoes and put them into a baking tray. Cover them with grated ginger and chilli flakes to taste and put into the oven for the last 45 minutes of cooking, put the knob of butter in the tray to prevent from sticking.

Baste the chicken halfway through cooking and if the vegetables look dry, add a splash of water to the tray.

When cooked, take the tray out of the oven and transfer the chicken to a board to rest for 15 minutes or so before serving.

Sadie Kaye

My recipe is for **Barack Obama**
(and **Ronnie Corbett**!).

Obama Fish Pie:
CAN WE COOK IT? "YES WE CAN!"

Ingredients

For the filling

350g/12oz mixture of fresh deboned monkfish

350g/12oz smoked haddock, skin removed

1 small onion, peeled and quartered

1 bay leaf

650ml/1 pint 3fl oz milk

For the spuddy top

1kg/2lb 2oz Maris Piper potatoes, peeled

Salt and pepper

50g/2oz butter

4 free range eggs

2 tbsp chopped fresh parsley

50g/2oz gruyère or cheddar cheese, grated

For the sauce

25g/1oz butter

25g/1oz plain flour

Pinch freshly grated nutmeg

Salt and pepper to season

Method

Pre-prep. Pre-heat the oven to 190°C/375°F/gas mark 5. Peel and chop the spuds into chunks. Boil eggs for 8 minutes, cool, peel and chop into quarters (along length). Chop parsley.

Poach the fish. Place fish pieces in wide pan, add onion and bay leaf and pour over 450ml/16fl oz of the milk. Bring milk to boil, reduce heat and simmer for 8 minutes, or until fish is just cooked. When that's done, take the fish out and break up into chunky pieces. Keep the milk that the fish was poached in, and put to one side, but discard the onion and bay leaf.

Make mashed potato. Boil spuds for 20 minutes. Drain water and let the spuds steam off excess water for a couple of minutes. Add butter to pan and mash spuds until smooth. Add remaining milk to spuds (NOT the set-aside poaching milk) and mash in. Season with salt and pepper and a bit of freshly ground nutmeg. Keep spuds aside for moment.

Make white sauce. Melt butter in pan, stir in the flour and cook for 1 minute over moderate heat. Let the flour/butter cook off and then cool before adding the fish poaching milk. As you add, whisk and then simmer for 1 to 2 minutes, stirring, until you have a smooth, slightly thick sauce. Season with salt and pepper.

Finish pie. Arrange the quartered eggs evenly over the fish. Sprinkle parsley over the lot, pour and evenly distribute the sauce over the fish and eggs. Delicately paddle the mashed potato over the top of the sauce by spooning potato onto the outer perimeter of the dish, finishing in the middle, and sprinkle with grated cheese.

Bake the dish. Place in oven and cook for 35 minutes until golden on top.

Serve fish to your dishy wish-date. Serve with "Nobel" peas. DON'T be tempted to crack jokes about spilling oil on fish!

Small Fish Pie for Ronnie Corbett
Exactly the same but using a quarter the quantity. Watch out for funny bones. Start with Small Bites. Follow with shortbread.

Lorraine Kelly

My mum **Anne Kelly** is my role model.

She is always sunny and cheerful and her glass is always half full. She had me when she was just seventeen and taught me to read and write before I went to primary school.

She has always supported me in everything I do. She is very caring and helpful and no-one has a bad word to say about her, which says it all!

Lorraine Kelly's Mum's Chicken Soup

Ingredients

*2 pieces uncooked chicken
(legs are best)*

4 or 5 carrots

1 small turnip

4 potatoes

1 large leek

4 sticks celery

Parsley

Method

Put the chicken in a pot, cover with water and cook. (Don't use too much water, you can always add more later if you have to.) Chop up the carrots, turnip, potatoes, leek and celery. (Chop up the leek and celery finer than the other chunks, making sure the celery isn't 'stringy'.)

Put the veg in the pot with the chicken and water as you cut them up. Cook on a high heat until all the vegetables are in the pot, then turn it down and let the whole thing simmer for an hour. Add salt and pepper to taste.

When the vegetables are ready (just taste them, you'll know when they are soft enough), take the chicken pieces out and mash the vegetables. Skin the chicken, then chop up the meat and put the pieces back in the pot. Finally, chop up and add the parsley.

This is full of goodness and really filling.

" Lorraine's Cooking Tip

This is not only comforting, filling and healthy – it also tastes fantastic, even though I can never get it as good as my mum does. It is a good idea to make a pot on Sunday night and it will last you through the week. It's perfect for lunch; just don't overdo the crusty bread and butter! "

Felicity Kendal, CBE

I would like to cook for **Oprah Winfrey** because she would make me laugh and I hope would not mind that I am a lousy cook. I think she is a role model for millions – she certainly is for me. I would cook the following…

Chicken Goujons served with Baked Potato with Butter or Sour Cream and Chives, Green Beans and a small mixed salad of Baby Gem Hearts

Ingredients

8 chicken goujons – breaded

2 handfuls green beans

2 small baking potatoes

2 baby gem lettuce

5 garlic cloves

Olive oil – the best you can get for cooking

2 lemons

Cup sour cream

Butter

Small fistful chives

Sea salt

Freshly ground pepper

Mint (3-4 leaves)

Method

In a large, heavy bottomed frying pan, pour olive oil to cover base and drop garlic cloves into it. When the oil sizzles, place the goujons in with space between. Sprinkle with salt and pepper. After about 4 to 5 minutes, turn over the goujons (using tongs) and again sprinkle the cooked side with salt and pepper.

Then put in three knobs of butter and after a few minutes, squeeze half a lemon over goujons. Then turn heat down and keep turning the goujons over until both sides are crispy brown. These will take at least 10 to 12 minutes to cook, maybe more, depending on thickness of goujons.

Cook washed topped and tailed green beans in salted water. Put in 3 to 4 leaves of mint halfway through. When boiled, drain and drizzle with best olive oil you have got. Serve with chicken and lemon wedges.

Before you start cooking the goujons, put potatoes in microwave for 10 minutes on a suitable plate. Put oven to 180°C/350°F/gas mark 4. When it's 30 minutes before serving, smear potatoes with olive oil and sea salt and place in oven.

Time this to go with the chicken and beans and serve with butter or sour cream and chives.

For the gem salad, you will need to cut them into four and drizzle over olive oil and lemon juice, salt and pepper.

Serve goujons with lemon cut in half to squeeze and, of course, tomato ketchup to dip chicken into and/or mayonnaise if you feel greedy!

Jemma Kidd

My role model would be **Estée Lauder** because she was the ultimate beauty entrepreneur; she was a forward thinking beauty genius.

Pan Grilled Sea Bass with Herbed Butter, Seasoned Vegetables and New Potatoes

Ingredients

4 fillets with the skin on
Seasoned flour
Knob of butter
New potatoes
Mint leaves
Baby vegetables
Baby leeks and carrots
Lemon wedges

Herbed butter
2 tbsp chopped flat-leaf parsley
1 tsp fresh lemon juice
3½oz butter

Method

First cream the butter, add the chopped parsley and lemon juice. Shape into a roll and cover with greaseproof paper or clingfilm and put in the fridge to get hard.

Boil some water and cook the new potatoes, add some mint leaves to the water if you like for extra taste.

Steam baby vegetables, baby leeks and carrots until slightly crunchy. Once cooked, keep warm and season.

Gently dust the fillets in seasoned flour so they have a light covering on both sides. On a medium heat add the knob of butter to the pan, be careful you don't burn it. Place the skin side down first, let it brown gently, once brown flip over and again cook gently so it turns a lovely golden colour.

Once cooked, place the fish on a warm plate with lemon wedges and the herbed butter, add the vegetables and potatoes and season.

Helen Lederer

My role model would be **Joyce Grenfell**. I would love to chat to her about how England was when she was in her prime and how she got her ideas and who she wrote with. I admire her for being unconventional for the times she lived in and striking out on her own with her own material.

She was good-hearted and entertained people in a unique and original way. More of those people please!

I would cook a mix of flavours as I'm sure Joyce was a complex character deep down.

Roast potatoes with a twist, salsa and yummy sticky chicken ... maybe a few rocket leaves on the side.

Lemon Roasted Potatoes

Ingredients

1kg baby new potatoes

4 tbsp olive oil

2 lemons grated zest of both and juice of 1

1 tsp sugar

Black pepper

Method

Cook 1kg potatoes in salted boiling water for 5 minutes, drain, transfer to roasting tin.

Whisk olive oil, sugar, salt and pepper, lemon juice and zest, pour over potatoes and toss well.

Roast at 190°C/375°F/gas mark 5 for 20 to 30 minutes.

Avocado Mango Salsa

Ingredients

1 mango diced

1 avocado halved

½ red onion

1 red chilli

1 tsp lime juice

1 tbsp red wine vinegar

2 tbsp olive oil

1 tbsp finely chopped mint

Salt

Tabasco

Method

Combine everything and leave to stand for 30 minutes.

Honey Mustard Chicken

Ingredients

6 garlic cloves

3 tbsp honey

2 tbsp creamy Dijon mustard

2 tbsp soy sauce

1 tbsp lemon juice

1 tsp black pepper

8 drumsticks or chicken breasts

Method

Combine garlic, honey, mustard, soy sauce, lemon juice and pepper. Add chicken and toss to coat. Put in fridge, covered, for 1 hour.

Grill, turning every 3 minutes for 15 minutes, or oven bake for 20 minutes.

Choc hobnobs and mint tea to follow.

Gary Lineker, OBE

I would cook for **President Obama** because to get to the position he is in from his upbringing makes him very special! It would be incredible to hear the thoughts of the world's most powerful man.

Paella is my favourite meal, which I learnt to cook during my time spent in Spain when I was playing for Barcelona. I loved the life in Spain, learnt to speak Spanish and fully embraced the life there, even managing to learn how to cook one of their most famous dishes!

Paella

Ingredients
(for 6)

2 tbsp oil

1 onion – peeled and chopped

1 clove garlic – finely chopped

3 chicken joints – halved

8oz squid rings

1lb rice

½ tsp powdered saffron

½ tsp paprika

2 tsp tomato puree

1 tsp fresh parsley

1½pt chicken stock

Juice of ½ lemon

1lb mussels – frozen on the half shell and defrosted

4oz cockles

4oz whole prawns

Method

Heat oil in large frying pan and cook onion and garlic until soft.

Add chicken pieces and cook for 5 minutes.

Add squid rings and cook for 2 minutes, turning everything over.

Add rice and stir. Add saffron, paprika, tomato puree and parsley, and then add stock and lemon juice.

Bring to the boil, then turn down to simmer.

Add mussels and cockles and cook for 20 minutes or until rice is tender.

10 minutes before end of cooking time, add prawns.

Kenny Logan

I would love to meet and cook for **Nelson Mandela** as he's such an inspirational man.

I would cook Haggis, Neeps and Tatties followed by Sticky Toffee Pudding. Nelson Mandela is interested in people, their nationalities and traditions, so I am sure he would love to try some good old Haggis.

Haggis, Neeps and Tatties

Ingredients

Haggis

1.2-1.5kg haggis (look for the best quality you can find, it is now found in many butchers and supermarkets around the world, or order it in if you have to)

Tatties

600g mashing potato, peeled and roughly chopped

60ml milk

4 tbsp butter

A generous pinch of grated nutmeg

Maldon salt

Neeps

600g swede (turnip), peeled and roughly chopped

4 tbsp butter

3cm ginger, peeled and chopped or ground ginger

Maldon salt and freshly ground black pepper

Orkney Clapshot

Tatties and Neeps (equal quantities)

2 tbsp chives, finely chopped

Cooked kale, cabbage or spinach tossed in a little butter and season with a little salt and pepper

30ml whisky

Method

Haggis Place the haggis in a large saucepan and cover it with cold water. Bring the water to a strong simmer then reduce the heat to a gentle steady simmer and cover the pan. Leave the haggis to cook for 40 minutes per 500g.

Tatties Place the potatoes in a saucepan and cover them with cold water, bring the water to the boil then reduce it to a strong simmer. Leave the potatoes to cook for 20 to 30 minutes until they are tender. Drain the potatoes well and return them to the pan. Return the pan to the low heat and dry the potatoes for a couple of minutes. Add the butter and milk to the pan and mash the potatoes with a fork or potato masher. Add the nutmeg and a little salt to the potatoes and beat them to a smooth mash.

Neeps Place the swede (turnip) in a saucepan and cover them with cold water. Place the pan over a high heat and bring the water to a boil, reduce the heat to a strong simmer and leave the swede to cook for 20 to 30 minutes until they are tender. Drain swede and return them to the pan. Place the saucepan over a low heat and cook the swede to dry it out for a couple of minutes. Add the butter and ginger to the pan and cook them with the swede for a minute.

Mash the mixture with a fork or potato masher. Season the Neeps with a little salt and pepper and beat it until smooth.

Orkney Clapshot Mix together equal quantities of "Tatties and Neeps" with the kale, the whisky and the chives until well combined. Serve.

To Serve Haggis Remove the haggis from the pan and cut it open with scissors or a knife. Serve the Haggis accompanied with Tatties and Neeps or Orkney Clapshot and your choice of greens. Drizzle a little whisky over each serving of haggis (optional). Serve.

Kenny Logan

Sticky Toffee Pudding

For the pudding

150g/5oz dates, stones removed, chopped

250ml/9fl oz hot water

1 tsp bicarbonate of soda

60g/2¼oz butter, softened

60g/2¼oz caster sugar

2 free range eggs

150g/5oz self raising flour

For the toffee sauce

200g/7oz butter

400g/14oz brown sugar

Vanilla pod, split

Pre-heat the oven to 180°C/350°F/gas mark 4.

Mix the dates, bicarbonate of soda and the water together in a bowl and leave to soak for ten minutes.

In a clean bowl, cream the butter and sugar together until light and fluffy.

Still stirring the butter mixture, gradually add the eggs, making sure they are well mixed in.

Still stirring, gradually add the flour, then add the date mixture.

Pour the mixture into a 20cm/8inch square cake tin. Place into the oven and bake for 35 to 40 minutes, or until cooked through.

To make the sauce, melt the butter in a thick bottomed pan over a medium heat.

Add the brown sugar, vanilla pod and cream and stir well. Simmer for five minutes.

To serve, spoon out a portion of the pudding onto a plate and pour over the hot toffee sauce.

Bill Nighy

I want to cook for **Christopher Walken** because he is by a mile my favourite actor and because he is one of the rare people whose every one word and every move is poetic..

Fèves Au Lard Sur Un Toast Avec Marmite Sous

Lightly toast 2 slices of respectable bread whilst gently warming through the beans, turn off heat under the beans as you introduce the butter to the bread. A respectable amount of Marmite should then be applied, followed obviously by the beans. Sprinkle an irresponsible amount of pepper – no salt, over everything. Hopefully the radio will have been playing throughout this process and the newspaper already opened at the football page. Turn off the phone.

© John Shakespeare 2010

Liz McClarnon

My role model is **Dawn French** – I think she's a fascinating and genuine woman. I'd like to pick her brains about how she's dealt with fame, life and comedy. I've met her a few times but I reckon she'd go crazy for the risotto.

Butternut and Pancetta Risotto (Tash's fave)

Ingredients

2lb butternut squash

160g pancetta

2 tbsp each of butter and olive oil

340g onion; diced

1 tbsp garlic; minced

550g arborio rice

180ml dry white wine

1¾pts rich chicken or vegetable stock

340g freshly grated Parmesan

Zest of ½ a lemon

¼ tsp freshly grated nutmeg

Garnish chopped chives

Shaved Parmesan

Basil oil

Salt and pepper

Method

Peel the squash and remove seeds.

Cube into small ¼ inch dice. Set aside.

Heat the butter and oil together in a deep saucepan and sauté the onions, garlic and pancetta for about 2 minutes.

Add the squash and rice and continue to sauté and stir for 2 to 3 minutes longer.

Add wine and stir until absorbed.

Add stock in ½ cup increments stirring until absorbed.

Continue adding stock and stirring until rice is creamy on outside but has some texture to it.

Gently stir in cheese, zest, nutmeg and correct seasoning with salt and pepper.

Serve immediately in warm bowls, garnished with chopped chives, additional Parmesan and a drizzle of fresh basil oil, if desired.

Danny McGuire

My role model would have to be **Grandad** who sadly died in 2009. When I was young he introduced me to cricket and rugby, my two biggest passions. Throughout my rugby career he was always my biggest supporter, no matter what had happened on the pitch. He continued to play cricket in his later years, even bowling the opening over in a match when he was 86!

I have chosen a Thai dish as Thailand is my favourite holiday destination and this is the only dish I can recreate at home. I love all the different flavours in the soup and when I eat it at home it reminds me of the beach.

Tom Kha Kai
(chicken, coconut and galangal soup)

Ingredients

1 tin coconut milk

2 lemon grass stalks (bruised)

5cm piece of galangal (chopped into small pieces)

4 Asian shallots (or small ordinary shallots) crushed with flat side of knife

400g skinless chicken breast (diced)

2 tbsp fish sauce

1 tbsp of palm sugar

200g cherry tomatoes

150g button mushrooms (chopped into bite sized pieces if large)

3 tbsp lime juice

3-5 bird's-eye chillies (seeded and finely sliced)

Coriander leaves to garnish

Method

Put the coconut milk, lemon grass, galangal and shallots into a saucepan over a medium heat and bring to the boil.

Add the chicken, fish sauce and palm sugar and simmer, stirring constantly for 5 minutes or until the chicken is cooked through.

Add the tomatoes and mushrooms and simmer for 2 to 3 minutes. Add the lime juice and chillies in the last seconds. Taste and then adjust the seasoning (fish sauce – salty, palm sugar – sweet, chillies – hot, lime juice – sour) if necessary. This dish is not meant to be overwhelmingly hot, but to have a sweet, salty, sour taste. Garnish with coriander leaves and serve with jasmine rice.

Sophie
Michell

I would say my role model is my mother,
Chris Michell, as she brought my brother
and I up completely on her own, both
financially and physically, all the while
keeping her career as a flutist going. We
travelled lots, I never wanted for anything
and we always felt supremely loved.

She is an independent and strong minded
woman and has pushed my brother (who
is a doctor now) and I to do as much as
possible with our lives.

Vine-leaf wrapped Chicken with Ricotta, Pine Nut and Mint Stuffing

Ingredients
(for 4)

250g reduced-fat ricotta cheese or the Greek cheese called Mizithra

50g toasted pine nuts

50g sultanas

3 tbsp fresh mint leaves, chopped

Zest one lemon

4 free range skinless boneless chicken breasts, about 125g each

12 vine leaves (these can be bought in jars in good delis or some supermarkets)

Sea salt and freshly ground black pepper

To serve

1 red onion, thinly sliced

1 fistful picked flat-leaf parsley leaves

2 tbsp olive oil

1–2 tbsp lemon juice

1 large aubergine

2 garlic cloves, thickly sliced

Method

Pre-heat the oven to 200°C/400°F/gas mark 6. Mix the ricotta, sultanas, pine nuts, chopped mint leaves, lemon zest and seasoning together.

To prepare the onion salad, mix the onion slices with the picked whole parsley leaves and the oil and lemon juice. Season and set aside while you cook the chicken.

Place the chicken breasts on a very clean board and, using a sharp knife, cut through the middle horizontally, but not right through. This will make a butterfly shape when the chicken breast is opened up.

Press a quarter of the ricotta filling in the centre of a breast and fold the top flap of flesh to sandwich together like a sub roll.

Lay out 3 vine leaves so they overlap slightly. Place a stuffed chicken breast on top and fold in the sides to enclose, then roll up tightly to form a cylinder-shaped roll. Place join-side down in a shallow baking dish. Repeat with the other three breasts. Season lightly, cover loosely with foil and bake for 30 to 35 minutes until they feel firm when pressed with the back of a fork. Remove and leave to stand while you cook the aubergines.

Pre-heat a griddle pan until hot. Slice the aubergine into 1cm slices. Slice the garlic lengthways and rub onto both sides of the aubergine. Brush the aubergines lightly with olive oil and season. Cook the garlic-flavoured aubergines for 4 to 5 minutes on each side, getting lots of colour and making sure they cook right through. There is nothing worse than undercooked aubergine!

Arrange the aubergine slices on warmed plates. Slice each chicken breast in half on the diagonal and place on top of the aubergines. Spoon the onion salad around the chicken and serve.

Fabulous Food: Sexy Recipes for Healthy Living by Sophie Michell is published by Sphere (Hardback, £16.99)

Michelle Mone, OBE

I've always admired **Bill Clinton**.

Having met him, he is one of the most charismatic, gracious people I have ever come across and in my opinion one of the great engaging speakers of our time.

If I was cooking dinner for Bill I'd want my menu to showcase Scotland's finest produce, so I'd go for seared scallops with Stornoway black pudding to start, followed by an Aberdeen Angus fillet steak with triple cooked chips and asparagus for main course, and then a strawberry Pavlova for dessert.

Seared Scallops with Stornoway Black Puddings, Aberdeen Angus Fillet Steak with Triple Cooked Chips and Asparagus

Ingredients (for 4)

Seared Scallops with Stornoway Black Puddings

4 slices Stornoway black pudding

8 scallops

Chilli flakes

Black pepper

Salt

Salad

Vinaigrette

Ingredients (for 4)

Aberdeen Angus Fillet Steak with Triple Cooked Chips and Asparagus

4 steaks

Olive oil

30g butter

1 tbsp whole grain mustard

100ml red wine

8 medium Maris Piper potatoes

250g asparagus

Method

Fry four slices of Stornoway black pudding in hot oil to a slightly crisp texture.

Season 8 scallops with ground chilli flakes and black pepper and a little salt, sear in very hot olive oil until golden brown.

Place scallops on top of the black pudding and place on a bed of a mixed leaf salad and finish off with a drizzle of fresh vinaigrette dressing – home made of course.

Method

Simply fry 4 seasoned steaks in a hot pan with 1 tablespoon of olive oil. Once seared, reduce heat and cook to desired level (medium/rare etc). Once cooked, remove from pan, add 30g of butter and 1 tablespoon whole grain mustard to pan and heat with 100ml of red wine. Reduce sauce and pour over steak when serving.

For chips cut and rinse (well) 8 medium Maris Piper potatoes, boil for 3 minutes, dry, deep fry until starting to colour in medium to hot oil and then remove and dry again. Finish by deep frying again in very hot oil until golden brown and slightly crispy.

For asparagus rinse and boil 250g for 3 minutes, drain and serve tossed in butter and black pepper.

Anton Mosimann, OBE

One of my early heroes was **Cassius Clay**, even before he became Muhammad Ali. October 30 1974; I remember staying up all night to watch the so-called 'Rumble in the Jungle' when Ali fought George Foreman and beat the champion. It was so exciting, as it was probably one of the earliest live broadcasts of a boxing match and because of the time difference we could watch it after service! He has always been an inspiration to me, because of his sheer determination to win; his achievements were absolutely incredible and he proved that whoever you are, anything is possible if you want it badly enough. Even today, although he is so ill, he has such dignity and a great presence.

I met him, many years ago, he was one of those people that did not disappoint. It was a really exciting moment to meet such an outstanding sportsman. He literally came off the plane and came directly to the kitchen and we had lunch together; the dish that I have chosen is in fact exactly what I cooked for Muhammad Ali all those years ago.

Tournedos of Beef with Four Peppers

Ingredients
(for 4)

3g whole dried green
peppercorns

3g whole red peppercorns

1g white peppercorns

1g black peppercorns

4 x 150g fillet of beef

100ml oil

Salt

Peppercorn Sauce

100ml reduced veal stock

20g sliced shallots

20ml red wine

20ml Port

Pinch of rosemary

1 tbsp crushed black peppercorns

20ml Cognac

100ml double cream

2 tbsp green peppercorns in brine

Method

Lightly crush all the peppercorns and place on a plate.

Season with salt and press one side of the steak into the crushed pepper. Seal beef in a hot pan with some oil until golden brown. Cook in a hot oven to desired temperature.

Peppercorn Sauce
Sweat shallots and rosemary with a little oil in a pan and brown lightly. Deglaze the pan with the wines and reduce until sticky. Add the veal stock, bring to the boil, skim and simmer for about 20 minutes. Allow the sauce to become thicker and pass through a fine sieve.

Sauté the peppercorns in a hot dry pan for a few seconds and flambée with Cognac. Add the brown sauce and cream, simmer for a few minutes to the desired taste. Pass through a fine sieve. The colour of the sauce should be 'café au lait.' Add more cream if needed to achieve the café au lait colour.

To serve, heat the green peppercorns and sprinkle in the sauce.

Jean-Christophe Novelli

Michelin and 5AA Rosette award-winning chef, and "the nation's favourite French chef": My role model would be **Detective Columbo** (from the popular TV series, played by Peter Falk). His ways and methods of deduction are brilliantly unpredictable. He is unassuming, often underestimated, but always gets his man (or woman!).

I was supposed to meet Peter Falk on my way to be a guest on the Ellen Degeneres show in the US, but sadly because of the airline strike I wasn't able to go. Another time maybe!

As Columbo is of Italian descent, I would cook him my famous tomato sauce – it goes brilliantly with pasta, vegetables, fish or meat, or as a base for a delicious curry sauce.

© Noel Murphy 2010

Grandma Louise's Tomato Sauce

Ingredients

6 beef tomatoes halved or
4 x 400g cans chopped tomatoes

4 star anise

Vanilla pod

Sea salt and cracked black pepper
to season

Runny honey, to taste

2 sprigs fresh thyme

1-2 bay leaves

Cumin seeds

Fennel seeds

Infusion

Fresh garlic

1 bunch fresh basil

Extra virgin olive oil

Method

Heat up a pan and add the anise, cumin, fennel and vanilla. Add the halved tomatoes (or tinned) and allow them to start to cook, season with salt, pepper and honey if required.

Press them gently with a masher to help them to release their juice. As they cook down, the skins can now be easily removed with a fork or left in.

Reduce the heat down to just simmering and continue for about 1½ to 2 hours until you have a thickened paste. This slow evaporation of the moisture from the tomatoes will produce a deep colour concentrated flavour without any bitterness.

When all the moisture is removed add the cracked garlic and basil.

Combine with the warm paste and finish with a good amount of olive oil to finish the infusion. Allow to cool before storing ready for use.

To make a tomato sauce, add a touch of water. This may seem strange because you have taken so much care to remove all the water only to add it back in. Only now are you in control of the sauce because you have reduced the consistency and the flavour.

" Jean's Cooking Tip

Always taste the tomatoes uncooked to determine their natural sweetness before you add the honey or sugar.

Slow cooking is the trick to this recipe by evaporating all the water to concentrate the flavour.

The amount of garlic to infuse with greatly depends on its strength; again make your own judgment.

The infused oil on top of the paste can be used to coat fish or chicken etc. or simply leave the oil to infuse with the cumin and vanilla for a week.

Great for serving with pasta and cooked meats.

"

Sasha Parker and Korin Nolan

Kylie Minogue is an idol to us, as she represents everything a modern-day woman should be! Strong, independent and beautiful both inside and out, what is there not to admire? Not only a fantastic businesswoman and role model, but even during her illness – probably the hardest challenge of her life – she still had a presence we all envied.

Kylie is truly inspirational for women everywhere, and we would like to cook her our chilli and ginger fillet beef with wild rice; not only is it a fairly healthy choice but it's pretty damn delicious too... with just the right amount of spice, just like our Miss Minogue! It's fabulously easy to cook, even a busy woman like Kylie would have no trouble rustling this tasty number up for a loved one or lunch with the girls! Perfection!!

Chilli and Ginger Fillet Beef with Wild Rice

Ingredients (for 2)

1 carrot, peeled and sliced lengthways

2 fillets of beef

4 tbsp of sesame oil

8 tbsp of dark soy sauce

3cm piece of fresh ginger, peeled and grated

1 long red chilli, deseeded and finely chopped

120g mixed wild and basmati rice

1-2 tbsp olive oil, for frying

3 spring onions, finely chopped

2 tbsp of pine nuts

Method

First, marinate your beef fillets. Place the beef in a shallow dish or bowl and combine with the carrot, sesame oil, soy sauce, grated ginger and chilli, cover, and refrigerate for at least one hour. Don't leave for more than 2 hours however, or the beef will become too salty.

Meanwhile, bring a saucepan of water to the boil and cook the rice according to the instructions on the packet. Drain, and set aside.

Heat a frying pan over a medium heat and fry the spring onions and pine nuts in the olive oil for 3 to 4 minutes. Mix these in with the rice.

Next, remove the beef from the marinade. Heat a non-stick frying pan over a medium to high heat and fry the beef for about 5 minutes, being sure to seal it well on all sides.

Before the beef cooks through, add the marinade to the pan and cook for a further few minutes, allowing the marinade to reduce slightly.

Remove from the heat.

Take the beef out of the pan, slice thinly and arrange on a serving plate. Spoon the rice into clean martini or cocktail glasses and press down, then turn out onto the plate to form a pyramid shape next to the beef. Drizzle over the marinade and serve.

Tricia Penrose

My role model is **Madonna** as I have always been a huge fan. I used to go to all her concerts and although I have never managed to actually meet her, we did record in the same studio on alternate days when I was recording "Where Did Our Love Go" with Simon Cowell and she was recording "Evita".

So I guess you could say that the closest I have ever been to her was sharing the same coffee mug!!

I would therefore love to have her round for dinner and I would cook her traditional 'Scouse Stew' to give her a true taste of my native Liverpool.

Scouse Stew

Ingredients
(for 6)

*900g/2lb neck of lamb, cubed
(remove fat first)*

*450g/1lb stewing or braising steak,
cubed (remove fat first)*

*600ml/1pt beef stock, plus extra
hot water for topping up*

Oil for frying

3 onions, peeled and sliced

*900g/2lb potatoes, peeled
and sliced*

*900g/2lb carrots or parsnips
or swede, peeled and cubed
(or a mixture)*

2 small beetroot, sliced

1 level tsp chilli powder

Seasoning to taste

1 tbsp fresh thyme

Method

Pre-heat the oven to 160°C/325°F/
gas mark 3.

Heat a small amount of oil in a large
heavy-based pan (or, alternatively,
use a metal casserole dish).

Seal the beef and lamb in the hot oil,
turning often. As the meat begins to
brown, add the onions, and cook for
5 minutes whilst stirring often.
Place the sealed meat and onions
into a casserole dish and then add
all the other ingredients except the
salt (this will be added at the end to
ensure it does not toughen the meat).

Add to the casserole dish enough hot
water to just cover all the ingredients.
Place a lid on top of the casserole dish
and cook in the centre of the oven for
4 hours, ensuring the vegetables are
cooked through.

Taste, and add the salt to adjust
the seasoning.

Jo Pratt

I'm not sure if this is an obvious choice for someone in my line of work, but **Delia Smith** is my role model. From an early age I pretended to be her by acting out cookery demonstrations for my family (I think dyed mash potato wrapped in lettuce leaves was a highlight!) and I like to think my career has followed a similar path to Delia's – I just hope it continues in the way hers has. She is the Madonna of home cooking that has the knack of reading the nation when it comes to what they want to cook at home.

If she was to come to my house for dinner, I would choose to cook something easy to prepare that I could leave in the oven until it was ready. That way I could spend more time picking her brain about how I'm eventually going to be on the board of my own football team.

Lazy Tray Baked Chicken

Ingredients
(for 4)

8 boneless and skinless chicken thighs

2 onions, each cut into 4-6 wedges

2 large carrots, peeled and cut into large chunks

500g new potatoes, cut in half

1 large red pepper, seeded and cut into chunks

8 cloves unpeeled garlic

4 stalks rosemary

4 tbsp olive oil

2 tsp paprika

Juice ½ lemon

1 lemon cut into wedges

150g smoked bacon lardons or pancetta

2½ tbsp runny honey

Method

Pre-heat the oven to 200°C (180°C Fan)/400°F/gas mark 6.

Roast the chicken pieces for 10 minutes. Then toss everything together, apart from the honey in a roasting tray and season with salt and pepper. Place on the hob over a high heat and turn the chicken and vegetables around for a couple of minutes. Arrange the chicken so it is snuggled into the vegetables and then place in the oven for 30 minutes, turning the food a couple of times.

After the 30 minutes, drizzle over the honey and cook for a further 15 to 30 minutes.

Serve two chicken thighs, lots of vegetables and plenty of the sticky juices per person onto warm plates. That is it!

I love the simplicity of this recipe – minimal preparation, minimal washing up, but maximum flavour. There is no need for anything else to be served with this, unless you are really missing your greens, in which case a portion of tenderstem broccoli, or even a green salad, would be lovely.

Leon Pryce

Hi, my name is Leon Pryce and I play rugby for St Helens. My Idol growing up was **Ellery Hanley**.

I watched Ellery from being a young kid when he played for Wigan and his skill, dedication and natural ability was inspiring. Ellery Hanley came from a working class background and became what I class as the first real professional Rugby League player.

I still think he would give any player a run for their money even in today's game. He is the finest player I have ever seen and that is why he is my sporting Idol. I would cook him....

Chicken Curry (West Indian style) served with Rice and Peas

Ingredients (for 4)

4 diced skinless chicken breasts

1 tbsp vegetable oil

1 handful chopped coriander

1 onion, finely chopped

1 garlic clove, finely chopped

1 chopped spring onion

3cm long piece of root ginger, finely chopped

1 red chilli, deseeded and finely chopped

1 tbsp mild curry paste

400ml can coconut milk

1 large mango, cut into 1cm cubes

350g long grain rice

130g can kidney beans (drained and rinsed)

Method

The peas in this traditional West Indian dish are actually kidney beans, not green peas.

Heat the oil in a frying pan then add the chopped onion, garlic, and chilli and fry for a couple of minutes until the onions are browning.

Add the chicken to the pan and cook until the outside of the chicken is white.

Next, add the curry paste and ¾ of the can of coconut milk (you can use a low fat version if you prefer). Stir, and let simmer for 25 minutes, adding the coriander and mango for the last 5 minutes.

During the simmering, cook the rice as per the packet instructions. When almost ready, add the remaining coconut milk and the kidney beans. Allow to thicken slightly, then, when ready to serve, drain rice and spoon onto plates.

Spoon the curry on top, then garnish with the chopped spring onions.

Michael Riemenschneider

www.michael-riemenschneider.com

My role model is my grandmother **Wilma**, who inspired me from a young age and got me into food with her passion for ingredients and how she was always cooking.

From these moments I took her passion on board. Nowadays I combine my modern approach to cooking with her old ways of slow cooking. She, by all means, is my true food hero. Sadly, she died of cancer a few years ago now, but her passion stays with me.

Pan Seared Salmon and Beetroot Pearl Barley Risotto

Ingredients (for 2)

Pearl Barley

1 tbsp shallots – finely chopped

1 tbsp olive oil

1 thyme sprig – whole

1 garlic clove – cut in half

8 dessert spoons pearl barley

125ml beetroot juice

4 tbsp white wine

2 tsp cold butter

Salmon

2 x 180g salmon fillets – portioned

2 tbsp olive oil

2 tsp cold butter

Salt and white pepper for seasoning

6 leaves of basil

Method

Pearl Barley

Sauté shallots, thyme and garlic in olive oil, add the barley – salt and pepper – add white wine – reduce heat – add beetroot juice bit by bit – cook slowly for approximately 25 minutes, take out the garlic and the thyme.

Add cold butter.

Season with salt and pepper.

Salmon

Place a non-stick pan on the stove, add the oil, heat the pan till smoking point.

Score the salmon skin with a sharp knife, with three little cuts against the grain of the salmon, not too deep, just literally cracking the skin.

Place the salmon fillets into the pan by placing the salmon away from you into the pan. Reduce heat, wait till skin starts to crisp up on the sides, cook for about 3 minutes till golden brown.

Add butter, flip the salmon on its flesh side and take the pan off the heat, add the basil leaves, and let rest in the warm basil butter.

Place the beetroot risotto onto a plate, forming a hole in the middle, and place the salmon onto it. Playfully arrange some beetroot halves around the plate and serve with some sea salt on the top of the salmon.

> ❝ **Michael's Cooking Tip**
>
> For the perfect fish: Cook it on the skin side over a high heat with a little oil, until golden, and then turn off the heat and add butter so the fish rests in the melting, bubbling butter. ❞

William Roache, MBE

My role model would be any **guru**, **swami**, or **holy man** who has risen above his ego to his superior and spiritual self. An enlightened being who radiates love.

Goat's Cheese and Mushroom Tartlets with Avocado Salad

Ingredients
(for 4)

For the tartlets

375g puff pastry – ready rolled

300g mixed wild mushrooms

1 garlic clove, finely chopped

2 shallots, finely chopped

*150g goat's cheese –
cut into 8 slices*

1 tbsp butter

2 tbsp chopped flat-leaf parsley

For the salad

*2 avocados – stones removed
and sliced lengthways*

*6 vine ripened tomatoes,
cut into quarters*

½ red onion, sliced into rings

2 tbsp olive oil

20ml fresh lemon juice

*1 tbsp pine nuts, lightly fried
until golden*

20g shaved parmesan cheese

Method

For the tartlets

Heat the oven to 200°C/400°F/
gas mark 6.

Cut the pastry into 4 quarters and place on a greased baking sheet. Score the pastry 1cm from the edge, all the way around, but don't cut all the way through. Set aside.

Heat the butter in a frying pan and sauté the chopped mushrooms, shallots, garlic and parsley for 3 to 4 minutes, allowing the juices to evaporate (you don't want the mixture to be soggy).

Add a spoonful of the mixture to the centre of each pastry quarter. Season well. Place in the oven for 15 minutes. Remove, and top with 2 goat's cheese slices. Place back into oven for 5 minutes until pastry is golden, and cheese melting.

For the salad

Toss all the ingredients, except the cheese and pine nuts, in a bowl.

Sprinkle the cheese and pine nuts on top of the salad and serve.

William Roache, MBE

Tomato, Red Onion, and Basic Bruschetta

Approx. 20 cherry tomatoes, halved

½ red onion, finely chopped

3 tbsp olive oil

2 tbsp balsamic vinegar

Balsamic glaze to drizzle

2 peeled garlic cloves, cut into halves (so can be rubbed on the bread)

Ciabatta bread, carved into four, 1cm thick slices

Fresh basil leaves to garnish

Mix together the tomatoes, onion, 2 tbsp of the oil, and the balsamic vinegar in a bowl. Cover and refrigerate.

Grill or toast the carved bread, then rub each slice with the cut side of the halved garlic cloves.

Place a large spoonful of the tomato and onion mixture onto the toasted bread. Top with torn basil leaves, and drizzle with balsamic glaze and the remaining olive oil.

Nicholas Owen

My role model would have to be **Isambard Kingdom Brunel**, the Victorian Engineer, the best of his age, who inspired so much of the best in the railways in this country. As a railway lover, I revere him, and his no-nonsense, buccaneering ways.

Scrambled Eggs

I could only manage reliably to cook him scrambled eggs... whisk at least three in a deep bowl... pour into a hot pan, add a splash of milk, and a generous knob of butter, and keep whisking with a wooden spoon until all is fluffy.

He has a choice of toast or smoked salmon to go with it.

And I would insist he smokes one of his beloved cigars, during the meal if he wished to!

© John Shakespeare 2010

Levi Roots

Peter Jones is one of my role models because he is an excellent businessman, and of course he spotted what I always knew would be a wise choice when he invested in me! So I would cook him a big meaty dish like my honey, grenadine and ginger roasted lamb with pomegranate and mint salad.

Honey, Grenadine and Ginger Roasted Lamb with Pomegranate and Mint Salad

Ingredients

3kg (6lb 8oz) leg of lamb
8 tbsp grenadine
10 tbsp runny honey
Juice of 3 limes and zest of 2
8 garlic cloves, finely chopped
Leaves from 8 sprigs of thyme
2 tsp ground cinnamon
2 tsp ground ginger
Salt and pepper

For the salad

1 small red onion
(very finely sliced)
Seeds from 2 pomegranates
30g (1oz) mint leaves
2 tbsp lime juice
6 tbsp extra virgin olive oil
Salt and pepper

Method

Wash the lamb and pat it dry with kitchen paper. Using a small, sharp knife, make incisions all over the meat. Mix all the other ingredients to make a marinade and spread it over the lamb, making sure some goes down into the incisions.

Cover with clingfilm and put in the fridge overnight. Turn the lamb over once or twice.

Remove the lamb from the fridge and allow it to come to room temperature.

Pre-heat the oven to 220°C/425°F/gas mark 7. Put a sheet of foil big enough to go all around the lamb in a roasting tin, lay the meat on top and season all over. Pull the foil up around the leg to almost cover, leaving it open slightly at the top so steam can escape.

Cook the lamb in the pre-heated oven for 15 minutes, then turn it down to 180°C/350°F/gas mark 4 and cook for a further 2 hours.

Open the foil after an hour so that the outside gets a lovely dark glaze, but pull it over again to cover if the honey starts to burn. Baste every so often with the juices and any leftover marinade.

When the lamb is cooked through, pull the foil up round it again, cover it with tea towels and leave to rest for 20 minutes before carving.

Make the salad just before serving by simply tossing all the ingredients together.

Serve the lamb with the cooking juices and the salad.

Extracted from Caribbean Food Made Easy with Levi Roots, published by Mitchell Beazley, priced £17.99.

Zoe Salmon

My role model is my **mummy** and I would cook her all the dishes she used to cook me. My favourites are her shepherd's pie and rhubarb crumble and also chocolate cake. They could never be as nice as hers but I can always try!

Pasta Delight!

Ingredients
(for 4)

3 chicken breasts

6 bacon rashers

1 red onion

1 garlic clove

1 yellow pepper (or your favourite colour of pepper!)

1 jar of green pesto sauce or red – whatever you fancy!

Pasta (wholemeal for the healthy option!)

Olive oil

Salt and pepper

Method

Chop the onion, garlic, peppers and cube the chicken.

Put the pasta on to boil with plenty of salt and a splash of olive oil.

Add the chopped onion and garlic to warm olive oil in a pan or wok.

While they're sweating off, put the bacon under the grill to cook while everything else is cooking in the pan.

When the onions have softened, add the cubed chicken with salt and pepper and leave to cook until the chicken starts to brown.

Once the chicken is starting to get some colour, add the peppers and leave to cook for a further 3 to 4 minutes.

When the bacon is cooked, remove from the grill and chop into short strips.

Drain off the pasta, add it, along with the chopped bacon, to the wok.

Add the jar of green pesto sauce and stir in well.

Give it 30 seconds or so to warm the pesto through, then serve.

Finishing touch – sprinkle some grated cheese (of your choice) over the top! I like medium cheddar or mozzarella! For the healthy option – don't bother!!

Voilà and Bon Appetit!

Arnold Schwarzenegger

This Austrian oven-baked pancake with raisins, served with powdered sugar and preserves, is truly a scrumptious treat that **my family** and I enjoy.

Kaiserschmarren

Ingredients
(Serves 2-3 as a dessert)

2 whole eggs

1 egg white

Pinch of salt

4 tbsp flour

2-3 tbsp milk or cream

2 tbsp raisins, preferably soaked in light or dark rum for 15 minutes, then drained

2 tbsp butter (total)

Powdered sugar for dusting

Cranberry sauce or berry preserves

Method

Pre-heat oven to 200°C/400°F/ gas mark 6.

Break egg and egg white into a mixing bowl. Beat with a wire whisk until well-blended and foamy. Whisk in salt, flour and milk or cream. Beat well, adding additional milk by driblets until a smooth batter is achieved.

Add batter to a medium non-stick frying pan over medium heat. In the batter melt 1 tbsp of butter and place in the centre of the oven.

When bottom of pancake is golden brown, flip it over with a spatula. Immediately place frying pan in pre-heated oven.

In 4 to 5 minutes, remove pan from oven. Pancake will have puffed slightly.

Using two rubber spatulas or wooden spoons, tear it into rough bite-sized pieces. Push pancake pieces against one side of the pan. Place pan back on a burner over medium heat.

In the "empty" half of frying pan, melt the remaining 1 tbsp butter, and then sprinkle the 2 tbsp sugar and the raisins over the butter, and let it bubble for a minute or two.

Quickly toss the torn-up pancake with the cooked butter and sugar, then turn out onto serving plates. Dust with powdered sugar and serve with preserves on the side.

William Simons

My role model is...**Yasmin Alibhai-Brown** – it's so good to see and hear a more recent arrival in the UK than myself talking such sense!

Tapenade and Baby Tomatoes on Toast

Ingredients

24 black Greek olives

100g of tinned tuna

2 heaped tbsp of capers

8 anchovy fillets (those that are in oil)

2 tbsp of french mustard

Juice of 1 lemon

Black pepper

2 coffee cups of olive oil

Method

Put the stoned olives into a mixer, add the tuna, capers and anchovies – WHIZZ – add mustard and olive oil slowly, and keep WHIZZING. Add black pepper and lemon juice. The final consistency should be as wallpaper paste.

Slice baby tomatoes in half. Slice through some country bread or sour dough and toast. Spread the tapenade mixture onto the toast, arrange the tomatoes on top, and sprinkle with fresh mint or basil if you have any to hand.

Kevin Sinfield

My role model growing up was legendary ex-Great Britain Rugby League captain **Ellery Hanley**, nicknamed the Black Pearl.

Growing up, playing the game at my local club, Waterhead ARLFC, Ellery was the player I admired with great respect. His immense pace, strength and agility when combined, created a world class athlete. It provided me with immense personal pride to eventually pull on the Leeds and Great Britain shirt and play in the position previously held by my predecessor.

The recipe I have chosen to prepare and serve to Ellery is Chicken Spirilli, a recipe I picked up from my favourite restaurant, Trio. It's a real favourite of mine and is a great source of carbohydrate.

Chicken Spirilli

Ingredients
(for 2)

1 tbsp olive oil

1 tbsp pine nuts

250g fusilli pasta

2 chicken breasts - diced

50g broccoli florets

30g mangetout

2 chopped carrots

30g mozzarella

30g parmesan cheese

4 basil leaves

Small handful flat-leaf parsley

Salt and pepper to season

Method

Heat the olive oil in a pan, and then add the diced chicken breasts.

Whilst the chicken is cooking, cook the pasta for ten minutes.

With five minutes remaining, add all the vegetables to a pan of hot water and boil.

When the chicken is almost cooked, add the pine nuts to the chicken pan and brown these.

Once the pasta and the vegetables are cooked, and you've checked the chicken is cooked thoroughly, drain the pasta and vegetables, and add to the chicken pan.

Add the basil leaves, chopped parsley, mozzarella, parmesan (retaining a small amount of shavings to garnish the finished dish with) and season well.

Serve the dish and garnish with the remaining parmesan.

Sinitta

I would invite **Oprah**!

I would make her my special egg-white, mozzarella and white truffle omelette. With a hint of black pepper and smidge of grated dry chillies!

The White Truffle Omelette

Ingredients

20g white truffle

8 eggs (use the whites only)

Salt and pepper

Coconut oil

A ball of fresh Mozzarella cheese cut into cubes

A generous pinch of dry chilli flakes

Method

Break the eggs and separate the whites into a bowl and whisk. Season with salt and pepper.

Rub a tiny amount of coconut oil onto a baking dish and pour in the egg mixture.

Place in a pre-heated oven at 250°C/500°F/gas mark 9, and it will rise like a cake!

Once it is fluffy and beginning to brown, remove it from the oven and ease it onto a plate with a spatula.

Grate the truffle over the omelette like a pizza and add the mozzarella and chilli flakes.

Serve with an icy glass of Angel white Champagne!

Carol Smillie

www.carolsmillie.tv

Jamie Oliver would be my role model. The work he does with young people is inspirational.

I would love to have Stephen Fry, Russell Brand and Dame Helen Mirren for dinner! I'd cook them a....

Chicken Szechuan Stir-fry with Jasmine Rice

Ingredients
(for 2)

2 chicken breasts

1 tbsp szechuan peppercorns

2 dried chillies

Jasmine rice (for 2)

Small bunch fresh coriander (stalks only – chopped)

1 garlic clove (sliced)

2cm fresh ginger (sliced)

½ medium red pepper (sliced)

Small bunch spring onions (sliced)

½ tsp cornflour

2 tsp sweet chilli sauce

Vegetable oil

Soy sauce

Salt

Method

Firstly, cut the chicken breasts into strips and place into a bowl to marinate in the soy sauce (leave approximately 30 minutes).

Next, put the rice on to boil in lightly salted water.

Meanwhile, heat a splash of vegetable oil in a wok, over a very high heat. Grind the chillies and the peppercorns in a pestle and mortar and add to the wok with a pinch of salt.

Add the marinated chicken strips to the wok and stir-fry until the chicken turns golden brown.

Return the wok to a medium heat and add the sliced garlic and ginger, the chopped coriander stalks, the sliced spring onions and red pepper, and fry for a further 30 seconds (making sure that the chicken is cooked through).

Sieve the cornflour into the wok, add the chilli sauce, a further tsp of soy sauce and stir.

When the rice is cooked, sieve and spoon into serving bowls. Pour the chicken mixture over the rice to serve and sprinkle with the remaining coriander leaves if desired.

Enjoy!

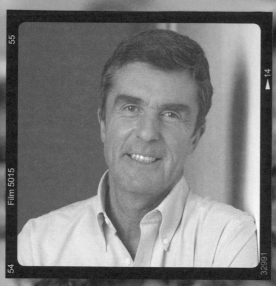

John Stapleton

Michael Parkinson is my role model.

I used to watch him, while I was doing my A levels, on a Granada TV local programme called "Scene at 6.30". It was a news current affairs programme not unlike GMTV and one of the first of its kind in the UK.

It was then I decided I wanted to go into TV, and Parky was my role model. I learned all about him – how he had gone straight from school into local newspapers and then Fleet Street before getting into telly and followed his example.

So he is to blame.

Quick Spicy Chicken

Ingredients

6-16 chicken breasts or thighs

*15fl oz thick single cream
(or part yoghurt/cream to make a
healthier dish!)*

6 tbsp Worcester Sauce

6 tbsp Mushroom Ketchup

*1 rounded dessert tsp Dijon
or mild mustard*

*8oz mushrooms, cleaned
and sliced (optional)*

Method

(A recipe from John Stapleton taught
to him by his wife Lynn Faulds Wood).

This is the quickest recipe in the world -
and no-one will guess what's in it!

Lightly oil a baking dish, arrange the
chicken in it and brush with oil.

Cook in a hot oven for 20 to 30 minutes
until nearly cooked.

Meanwhile, mix the cream/yoghurt,
sauces and mustard in a jug then pour
over the chicken, with the mushrooms.

Cook gently for a further 30 minutes
in the oven.

Guaranteed delicious!

Andy Street

Managing Director
John Lewis

Who I'd invite – **Ewan McGregor** – my favourite actor, as I think he's very down to earth, but has played some fascinating parts on stage and screen, including in the recent film Ghost.

What I'd cook - I suspect he'd like something really authentic. So I'd do Welsh Sea Bass straight from Cardigan Bay. It'd be perfectly fresh, with no messing. Just baked in the oven with a touch of lemon – simple for me but utterly unadulterated.

Always tastes best outside looking at the Welsh hills – Good for a Scotsman to enjoy!

Welsh Sea Bass

Ingredients

1 Sea bass
1 lemon (sliced)
Olive oil
Salt and pepper

Method

Pre-heat oven to 190°C/ 375°F/gas mark 5. Wash the fish and cut three slashes into one side. Place the fish onto a lightly oiled baking sheet with the slashes facing up. Insert the slices of lemon into the slashes. Bake for approximately 15 minutes per lb.

To be served with your own choice of vegetables.

Hayley Tamaddon

Here is the chocolate cake I used when I appeared on Britain's Best Dish. It's yummy and is a sure fire hit with all my guests!!

Daniel Whiston (Dancing on Ice skating partner 2010) is my role model, because he was an incredible teacher, patient, had a great sense of humour and put up with me for six months!!

Chocolate Cake

Ingredients

110g (4oz) butter at room temperature
220g (8oz) dark brown sugar
2 eggs
165g (6oz) self raising flour
55g (2oz) cocoa powder
½ tsp bicarbonate of soda
½ tsp baking powder
140ml (¼pt) sour cream

For the filling
5oz butter, at room temperature
165g (6oz) icing sugar
½ tsp ground coffee beans
Few drops vanilla essence
2 tbsp cocoa powder

For the frosting
200g (7oz) dark chocolate
140ml (¼pt) double cream
1 tbsp cocoa powder

For the chocolate curls
1 bar milk chocolate

Small jug double cream to serve

Method

Oven – 180°C/350°F/gas mark 4.

You will need 2 x 7½ inch round tins.

Butter the tins and line with greaseproof paper.

For the cake, cream together the butter and sugar using an electric whisk. Gradually beat in the eggs. Add the sour cream. Sieve together the flour, cocoa and bicarbonate of soda. Fold into the mixture.

Divide mixture into the two tins. Bake for 20 to 25 minutes.

For the curls, grate a bar of chocolate which has been left to reach room temperature. The chocolate bar needs to be warm but not to the point of melting.

For the frosting, melt the chocolate. Make the cocoa into a paste by adding hot water. Add the cocoa to the melted chocolate. Transfer to another bowl. Then pour double cream in and stir until thickened. Leave to cool so it goes harder.

Meanwhile, make the filling. Sieve icing sugar, coffee and cocoa into a bowl. Add butter and mix together until creamy.

Add a few drops of vanilla essence.

Once the cakes are cooled, slice the top off each cake to leave a flat surface. Put filling on one, sandwich together and frosting on top. Use a pallet knife to smooth over and decorate with the chocolate curls.

Danny Wallace

My role model, at least when it comes to cooking, would be my Swiss grandma, **Granny Breitenmoser**, who'd cook cakes and biscuits and delicious Swiss treats almost every day of her life.

It would be the other people in the village who would benefit, mainly, as they were invited round to try it, or would receive a knock at their door and see a pensioner on a moped with a freshly-cooked gift.

These guetzli are pretty simple to make, and we'd munch our way through them all Christmas... there are 200 different types of guetzli... I favour her hazelnut version...

Granny Breitenmoser's Christmas Hazelnut Guetzli

Ingredients

250g sugar

4 eggs

250g flour

100g unshelled, chopped hazelnuts

Method

Mix the sugar and the eggs together until they form a light foam.

Add the flour slowly as you mix, until what you're mixing becomes very smooth.

With a spoon, ladle a small heap of the mixture onto a buttered tray.

To every heap, add some heaped hazelnuts.

Bake in a medium hot oven for 15 to 20 minutes, or until the smell is just too tempting.

Granny Breitenmoser

Pete Waterman, OBE

When I think of 'role models', my mind takes me to people whose achievements I admire and respect and for this reason I would like to entertain the thought that I could sit around a table with **Isambard Kingdom Brunel**, who lived a relatively short life (1806-1859) but whose engineering achievements will be with us for eternity. I am in awe of all his work but particularly so when you think that all of it was achieved without the aid of modern day technology.

I wonder if he ever did something simple like fry eggs on the furnace of a steam engine and because of this I'm thinking that it would be great to invite him to my place for (almost) back to basics cooking with a 21st century twist! Assuming that he could arrange good weather (and I would put nothing beyond his capabilities) my menu for a BBQ would be as follows:

BBQ Tiger Prawns

Ingredients (for 4)

*Raw tiger prawns –
remove heads*

Garlic flavoured olive oil

Fennel seeds

Garlic salad dressing

Black pepper

Method

Mix all the ingredients for the marinade together. Wash and dry prawns thoroughly then cover them completely with the marinade. Cover and leave in fridge for a couple of hours. Remove from fridge 1 hour before you cook so that they are at room temperature. Chuck onto the BBQ and cook on both sides. They are cooked when they turn pink. Serve with a bit of tossed salad leaves and a slice of lemon.

Slightly Smoked Salmon with New Potatoes

Ingredients (for 4)

*Slightly smoked
salmon portions*

Lemon flavoured olive oil

Fresh dill

New potatoes

Method

Wash and dry the salmon fillets and without cutting into the salmon cut the skin. Cover the salmon in olive oil and dill and loads of black pepper on the skin then leave covered in the fridge until required. Put on the BBQ when you are eating the prawns. Does not take long to cook. Sear in both directions so you get a cross pattern (Isambard will like symmetry!). Serve with new potatoes.

BBQ Vegetables

Ingredients (for 4)

1 red pepper

1 yellow pepper

6 shallots

Tin of good tomatoes

Garlic oil

Few olives

Parmesan

Foil dish

Method

Drizzle oil onto the base of the foil dish then chuck in everything else bar the parmesan and mix well. Put the dish onto the BBQ before you cook the prawns. I am assuming that everyone uses natural BBQ's as opposed to gas ones so when I say put this on before anything else it's to encourage the charcoal – if you cheat and have a gas one then you won't need to!!

Take off the BBQ when it's all bubbling and add the parmesan in a good layer over the top. When you are ready, place this under a hot grill (you're in the kitchen now) just to finish off and to brown the cheese.

And for pud, strawberries and cream. Need I say more?

Stephen Webster

My role model in the kitchen is **Floyd** on fish and I would cook it for my wife as she cooks for me all the time.

Smoked Haddock Salad

Ingredients
(for 6)

1kg of undyed smoked haddock
(or cod)

2 bay leaves

Juice of 1 lemon

200g baby spinach leaves

1 cucumber

For the dressing

2 tsp horseradish sauce

1 tsp fresh grated horseradish
(if you can find some, if not add
a bit more of the sauce)

150g sour cream

1 tbsp mayonnaise

4 spring onions, finely chopped

Small bunch of dill, finely chopped

Salt and pepper

Method

Catch a haddock then smoke it (not literally, I tried this once and it laid heavy on my chest for weeks).

Place the smoked fish and bay leaves in a saucepan and cover with water. Vodka can also work.

Bring to boil and simmer for 5 minutes until cooked. That is about as long as it takes to enjoy a Marlboro Light.

Drain, discard the skin and bones into the cat bowl.

Break into chunks and sprinkle with lemon juice.

To make a dressing, combine all ingredients and mix well. Wives and girlfriends are good at dressing.

Cut the cucumber lengthways, remove seeds and slice. Mind your fingers.

In a large bowl, combine fish, cucumber, spinach and dressing. Check the seasoning and your pulse, serve immediately so the leaves stay crunchy.

Then drink a bottle of whatever takes your fancy.

Kevin Whately

My role model would be the actor, **Timothy West**, a marvellous and successful, yet rather undervalued performer, who has achieved pretty well everything in a distinguished stage and screen career, but at the same time grafts away tirelessly, championing regional and repertory theatre; drama students and schools, and giving generous professional and financial help to a hundred worthy causes.

The man is a National Treasure, and I would cook him a dish of my...

Kedgeree

Ingredients
(Serves 3-4)

1½lb of smoked cod or haddock (dyed or undyed)

½ pint milk (for poaching)

4 large eggs

1 tea mug of American long grain rice

1 sprig fresh parsley

Knob of butter

Fresh white bread

Salt, pepper, Worcester or Tabasco sauce to taste

Method

Poach the fish in a little simmering milk for 4 to 5 minutes.

At the same time, hard boil the four large eggs, and boil a tea mug full of American long grain rice until tender (about 10 minutes).

On a large plate, flake the fish fillets with a fork to get rid of any bones and skin.

Peel and shell the eggs, and chop into smallish cubes.

Chop a large sprig of parsley.

Drain the rice, and add to all the other ingredients in a large ovenproof bowl.

Add a generous knob of butter and reheat in a medium oven for 15 minutes.

Serve with fresh white bread, salt and pepper, Worcester/Tabasco sauce to taste.

This is an absolutely basic Kedgeree to which I can add a variety of other things if I fancy – lightly fried onion, bacon, peeled prawns, peppers and chillies.

© Dean Stockings

Toyah Willcox

My role model is **Anna Wintour**, from American Vogue, because she is feminine, powerful, successful and doesn't suffer fools, but at the same time is likeable.

Parmesan Soufflé

Ingredients

1 tbsp flour

1oz butter

½pt milk, warmed

2oz finely grated parmesan cheese

4 large egg yolks

5 large egg whites

Salt and freshly ground black pepper

Cayenne pepper

Method

Prepare the basic mixture by stirring one generous tablespoon of flour into 1oz of butter melted in a heavy saucepan. Gradually add just under ½pt of warmed milk, stirring until your mixture is quite smooth. Let this sauce cook very gently and slowly, stirring frequently, for close on 10 minutes.

Now stir in 2oz of finely grated parmesan cheese and then the very thoroughly beaten yolks of 4 large eggs. Remove the mixture from the heat, and continue stirring for a few seconds, add a seasoning of salt and quite a generous amount of freshly-ground black pepper.

Pre-heat the oven to 200°C/400°F/gas mark 6. Have the shelf placed fairly low in the oven, and a baking sheet on the shelf. Butter 1½pt soufflé dish.

Whisk the whites of the eggs in a large, dry and clean bowl, until they stand in peaks on the whisk and look very creamy. Tip half the whites on top of the basic mixture. With a palette knife cut them into it again, slowly rotating the bowl with your left hand, lifting rather than stirring the whole mass.

Add the remainder of the whites in the same way. All this should take only a few seconds and as you pour the whole mixture, without delay, into the dish, it should look very bubbly and spongy, but if the whites have been over-beaten or rammed into the main mixture with a heavy hand, it will already begin to look flat.

With a palette knife, mark a deep circle an inch or so from the edge, so that the soufflé will come out with a cottage-loaf look to the top. Put it instantly into the oven.

As to timing, it depends so much upon the size and type of both the oven and the dish. This soufflé is perfectly cooked at 200°C/400°F/gas mark 6 in 23 to 35 minutes.

Serve with warm, herby bread.

Richard Wilson, OBE

This recipe is dedicated to the memory of **Pina Bausch**. She was simply one of the great choreographers of the 20th century. She was instrumental in engendering my interest in contemporary dance and over the years I had the privilege of meeting and eventually dining with her. Despite the fact that she was extremely thin, she had a very sweet tooth and I'm sure would have loved Eton Mess.

Although it was always a pleasure to meet with her, she was an inveterate smoker so the meal was somewhat tinged with the knowledge that Pina would have to have her inter-course cigarettes.

So this recipe is given in fond remembrance of her.

Eton Mess

Ingredients

500g strawberries
300ml double cream
6 meringues
2 tbsp Grand Marnier

(The quantity of the ingredients can be varied according to taste.)

Method

Reserving a few strawberries for decoration, cut the remainder into halves and pour on the Grand Marnier.

Leave for about 2 hours.

Whip the double cream until firm but not too thick.

Crumble the meringues and mix with the strawberries and cream.

Serve in individual glass dishes and decorate with the reserved strawberries.

The meringue can go soft if left, so eat immediately. (You'll want to, anyway.)

Kim Woodburn

If he were still with us I would invite **Oscar Wilde** to dinner, for his ready wit, story telling and being an all round brilliant conversationalist.

Pork and Vegetables

Ingredients

*4 very lean boneless pork chops,
about three quarters of an
inch thick*

1 green and 1 red bell pepper

1 white onion

1000g of Passata

Method

Use a large saucepan. Lay the four chops side by side in the pan. Use the lowest heat setting and gently sear the chops. Turn them over after a few minutes and sear the other side. Pick up each chop with a pair of tongs and sear the edges, turning until all the edges have that "white" look.

De-core the peppers and cut into thin, round slices. Peel the onion and slice into thin round circles. With the chops side by side in the pan, layer the onion slices and the red and green peppers on top.

Pour the Passata over the top so that the chops/veggies are covered completely.

Cover the pan with a lid and simmer for 30 minutes. Then remove the lid and simmer for another 30 minutes until the sauce has reduced to a really thick consistency.

Serve with baked potato, new potatoes, rice or chips.

Can be frozen for future use.

Patrick Woodhead

On expedition, I usually have to eat awful bland food pretty much all the time. So, anything spicy is what gets me going and I loved the food when I was recently out in the Congo doing research for my next book.

As for dinner, I would invite **Muhammad Ali** round, as he has always been such an awesome character, brimming with charisma and inspiration. I would cook him Liboké de Poisson (Fish in Banana-Leaf) as I'd hope it'd remind him of the greatest fight of his career when he beat George Foreman in Kinshasa back in 1974. That was the Rumble in the Jungle and this fish can occasionally do that to your stomach!

Liboké de Poisson
(Fish in Banana-Leaf)

Ingredients

Banana leaves

2 to 4lbs of fresh fish (either whole, or cut into fillets, steaks, or pieces); in Africa freshwater fish are typically used

1 or 2 onions, fincly chopped

Juice of 1 or 2 lemons

Salt (to taste)

Black pepper (to taste)

Cayenne pepper or red pepper (to taste)

Oil (just a spoonful)

1 tomato, chopped and crushed (or canned tomatoes) (optional)

A few okra, chopped (optional)

Bunch of sorrel leaves (optional)

1 Maggi® cube (crushed) or a spoonful of Maggi® sauce (optional)

Method

If you are cooking a whole fish

Prepare a marinade by mixing together the oil, chopped onion, lemon juice, salt, black pepper, red pepper (and any optional ingredients you choose). Clean the fish, but leave the scales on, and cut a few gashes lengthwise on each side. Pour the marinade onto the fish and into the gashes. Let marinate in a glass dish for a quarter hour.

If you are cooking fish fillets, steaks, or pieces

In a glass bowl, combine all the ingredients (including the optional ingredients) except the fish and mix well. Add the fish and let marinate for a quarter hour.

Warm the banana leaves for a half-minute in a hot oven, on a grill, or in a pot of boiling water. This makes them easier to fold. Remove the centre rib of each leaf by cutting across it with a knife and pulling it off. Cut the ends off each leaf to form a large rectangle.

Fold the banana leaves to completely enclose the ingredients in a packet two or three layers thick. (Use something like the burrito folding technique. Depending on how many leaves and how much (or how many) fish you are cooking you may want to make more than one packet. Use ovenproof string to tie them closed.)

Cook the packets over an outdoor grill, or in an oven. (If using an oven, you may want to place some aluminium foil under them to catch drips.) Turn them every ten minutes. After half an hour carefully open the packet and check to see if the fish is cooked, if it is not, close the packet and continue cooking.

Serve in the packet with some Baton de Manioc (also called Chikwangue) or Fufu.

Antony Worrall Thompson

I'd pick **HRH Prince Charles** as my mentor/role model. He gets a lot of unwarranted flack from the press. He is a Prince, who has views on our country's architecture, the organic movement and many other relevant thoughts besides, rather than just a figurehead.

I know he's rather partial to mutton so I would present this offering to him, together with a 15 year old Laphroaig malt, which is reputed to be his favourite tipple. And no, I'm not angling for a knighthood – we'd just put the world to rights.

Herdwick Mutton with Creamy Onion Sauce, Buttery Mash

Ingredients (for 6-8)

3kg/6lb 8oz leg of mutton

3.5ltrs/6pts lamb stock
(or enough to cover meat)

1 bouquet garni

Salt

2 onions, peeled and stuck
with cloves

2 stalks celery, roughly chopped

1 tsp black peppercorns

2 carrots, peeled and diced

2 turnips, peeled and diced

Onion and Caper Sauce

3 onions, finely chopped

55g/2oz unsalted butter

3pts white sauce, made with
half milk and half lamb stock

The cooked vegetables

4 tbsp baby capers

4 tbsp chopped parsley

300ml/½pt double cream

For the Perfect Mash

1kg floury potatoes, peeled and
cut in chunks

115g/4oz unsalted butter

About 100ml/3½oz full fat milk, hot

4 tbsp double cream

½ tsp ground white pepper

1 level tsp salt

Method

Wipe the meat and trim off any surplus fat. Weigh the joint and allow 30 to 35 minutes per pound plus an extra 30 to 35 minutes.

Put the mutton in the pan, cover with the stock and add the bouquet garni and vegetables (carrots, celery and turnips). Bring to the boil, then reduce heat so that the water just murmurs and skim thoroughly from time to time throughout the cooking time. Season with salt when the mutton is half cooked.

Remove the meat from the stock and allow to rest in a warm place. Strain the stock, retaining the vegetables.

Meanwhile, gently sweat the onions in the butter for 20 minutes, being careful not to brown them. Set aside.

Pour white sauce into blender with the cooked vegetables and blend to a smooth liquid. Pour onto the sweated onions and gently stir in the cream and finally add the capers and parsley. Season to taste.

Carve the meat, place on a serving dish and coat with the onion and caper sauce. Serve with buttery mash and cabbage.

To make the buttery mash
Cover the potatoes with cold water and add salt, gently bring to the boil. Reduce heat and simmer until tender.

Drain well in a colander and return the potatoes in the colander to the pan and over a gentle heat, dry for a couple of minutes.

Mash with a traditional masher or ideally pass through a potato ricer.

Beat in the butter with a wooden spoon then gradually fold in the milk and cream, a little of each at a time. Season to taste.

NB: don't overbeat or the mash will become sticky and elastic.

Index

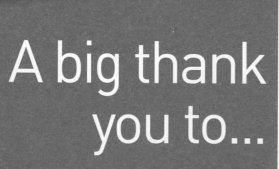

A big thank you to...

Leeds City College Hospitality & Culinary Arts staff and students for their help, professional advice and the production of dishes featured in this book for photographic purposes.

Leeds City College caters for those with a passion for food, serving up courses in Hospitality, Culinary Arts, Baking, Food Manufacture and Meat Technology.

As one of the country's leading culinary arts academies, it is renowned for its high quality training and is among only a select number of colleges to be awarded National Skills Academy status for Hospitality & Catering along with Bakery & Food Manufacture.

The College, the UK's third largest, trains budding young chefs as well as delivering professional courses to businesses, and works with Michelin Star restaurants throughout the country.

It also operates a number of on-site commercial outlets, including a bakery, butcher's shop and a popular public restaurant.

www.leedscitycollege.ac.uk

Leeds City College

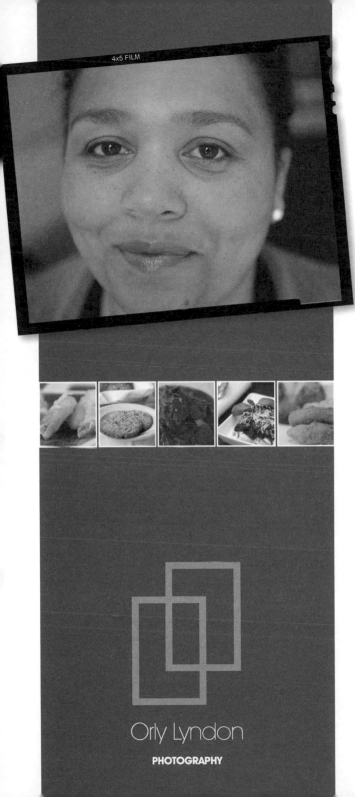

Orly Lyndon...

...is a freelance social and commercial photographer, living in Cheshire, specialising in Restaurant, Restaurant Interiors, situational food photography and intimate weddings.

For Commissions

www.orlylyndon.com

twitter olotwittwoo

For PR and Pro Bono requests

Contact the Jools Payne Partnership

I'm lucky enough to be surrounded by my heroes every day, in particular, my dad, my darling, my drewby, my girls and family, who make it possible for me to live my dream.

For those who are talented, believe in their dreams and are willing to work hard to accomplish it, The Prince's Trust offers that vital lifeline to building a brighter future; I wholeheartedly support them helping others to help themselves.

Orly Lyndon

Now we're cooking!

For us, just producing your communications isn't enough. We know we can really add value to your marketing by helping you to define and target your audience, develop bespoke communications and deliver through online or offline channels.

For a more efficient communications solution visit www.communisis.com

Communicate more profitably with

communisis